on track ...
Deep Purple

every album, every song

Steve Pilkington

Sonicbond Publishing Limited
www.sonicbondpublishing.co.uk
Email: info@sonicbondpublishing.co.uk

First Published in the United Kingdom 2018
First Published in the United States 2019

Reprinted 2020

British Library Cataloguing in Publication Data:
A Catalogue record for this book is available from the British Library

Copyright Steve Pilkington 2018

ISBN 978-1-78952-002-6

Typeset in ITC Garamond & Berthold Akzidenz Grotesk
Printed and bound in England

Graphic design and typesetting: Full Moon Media

Also by Steve Pilkington:

Black Sabbath - Song By Song
(Fonthill, 2017)
Perilous Journey: The authorised Gordon Giltrap biography
(Wymer Publishing, 2018)

Acknowledgements

I would firstly like to thank those band members who gave their time for interviews with me for the Classic Rock Society, which have been very useful in putting this book together: Glenn Hughes, David Coverdale, Roger Glover, Ritchie Blackmore.

Thanks to Stephen Lambe, for commissioning and faith, Jerry Bloom for massive Purple knowledge, Janet for patience and dog-wrangling, and all of those people who have done research before me!

Huge thanks to Doug Currie, Steve Richardson and Par Holmgren for photo contributions.

Finally thanks to all at the Classic Rock Society for the last ten years, without whom I wouldn't be who or where I am today (am I anywhere?).

And, of course, everyone who has passed through the ranks of Deep Purple and Rainbow: the founders of the feast...

on track ... Deep Purple

Contents

Introduction

The seeds of what would become Deep Purple were sown in 1967, when Middlesex-based guitarist Ritchie Blackmore and Leicester-born keyboard player Jon Lord joined forces with ex-Searchers drummer Chris Curtis, with a view to forming a band. Curtis had the idea of a band without a fixed line-up, whereby members could come in and out, and the project was thus christened 'Roundabout'. Almost immediately, the idea was thrown off course by the withdrawal of the erratic Curtis, and Lord and Blackmore set about getting the band on track themselves. The initial line-up was completed by bassist Nick Simper, who had been playing with Lord in a band called the Flower Pot Men, and temporary drummer Bobby Woodman. Vocalist Rod Evans was brought in after being spotted fronting a band called The Maze, whose drummer, Nottingham-born Ian Paice, came along with Evans, replacing the dissatisfied Woodman. Soon afterward, in early 1968, the band renamed themselves Deep Purple, and played their first UK show at The Lion pub in Warrington, Cheshire.

This first incarnation of the band lasted for a mere 18 months, though managing to record three albums in that time. In summer 1969, Evans and Simper were replaced by vocalist Ian Gillan and bassist Roger Glover, both from a band named Episode Six. This line-up quickly established themselves with a heavier rock direction, and became the most well-known line-up in most people's eyes. After a run of successful albums, inter-band feuding resulted in the departure of both Gillan and Glover in 1973, and the band were back to square one. Around this time the pattern of naming the Purple line-ups as 'Marks' (Deep Purple Mk I, Mk II, Mk III etc) became established. Unique among their contemporaries, it is unclear where this identification system originated, but it has been suggested that the first appearance was on a 1973 double compilation album called *Deep Purple Mk I And II*, which featured a disc dedicated to each line-up's output. Whatever the truth of the matter. The Mk III line-up needed to be finalised.

First into the fold was Staffordshire native Glenn Hughes, bassist / vocalist with Trapeze, who had achieved some success with the three albums he had played on. Quickly joining Hughes was 'unknown boutique salesman from Redcar' David Coverdale, who had, in something of a fairy-tale story, been plucked from obscurity after being persuaded to send in a demo tape. The band quickly got into the studio and recorded the acclaimed *Burn* album, and were an immediately successful rebuttal to the critics. The next album, *Stormbringer*, however, saw the band bringing in an overt funk/soul influence – primarily from Hughes – which led to the departure of the disenchanted Blackmore in 1975. Replacing him was American 'wunderkind' Tommy Bolin, who had turned heads with his time in the James Gang and with Billy Cobham, and the revitalised band recorded the excellent *Come Taste The Band* album. Alas, the hoped-for rebirth failed to materialise, with Bolin's soon-to-be apparent heroin problem seriously blunting his effectiveness on the road, and the band imploded inside a year, after a March 1976 show in Liverpool.

While Purple went on hiatus until a surprising reunion in 1984 (outside the scope of this book), Ritchie Blackmore immediately set about keeping the flame burning, forming Rainbow in 1975, using most of the band Elf as his initial backing band, including singer Ronnie James Dio. Rainbow recorded three stunningly successful albums with Dio as frontman until his departure in 1978 led to the introduction of the Hawaiian-shirted, cropped-haired Graham Bonnet as his unlikely successor. After Bonnet's sole Rainbow album, 1979's *Down To Earth*, this book leaves the story, but suffice it to say that Rainbow continued for a while until Purple abruptly reconvened, while Coverdale went on to enormous success with Whitesnake. For many, though, that first decade was where the true legends were forged, and thus it is that period that we will explore in these pages...

Shades Of Deep Purple

Personnel:
Rod Evans: vocals
Ritchie Blackmore: guitars
Jon Lord: keyboards
Nick Simper: bass guitar
Ian Paice: drums and percussion
Record Label: Parlophone (UK), Tetragrammaton (US)
Recorded May 1968, produced by Derek Lawrence.
UK release date: September 1968. US release date: July 1968.
Highest chart places: UK: Did not chart, USA: 24
Running time: 43:27

Album facts.

The album was recorded in May 1968, after the band returned from a Scandinavian tour under the name Roundabout. They changed their name to Deep Purple on the suggestion of Ritchie Blackmore, whose grandmother was reportedly very keen on the song of the same name – an easy-listening staple dating back to the 1930s. They completed the recording in a mere three days at Pye Studios in London, with production duties handled by Derek Lawrence, who went on to great success – with his stint as the man behind the production desk for the first three Wishbone Ash albums of particular note. The album gained immediate traction in the United States, largely on the back of the success of first single 'Hush', but by contrast went largely unheralded in their native UK, where it was only finally granted a release in the September of that year. The US record label was Tetragrammaton, whose intriguing name refers to the four letter Hebrew biblical name of God, from which the words Yahweh and Jehovah are derived. The label was co-owned by the comedian Bill Cosby. In the UK, the album came out on the Parlophone label, the EMI subsidiary which had released the early Beatles work.

Containing a roughly equal mix of covers and original material, the album is an enjoyable yet tentative musical step. Unlike the debut releases of Led Zeppelin or Black Sabbath, which would offer fully realised blueprints for their musical direction, *Shades Of Deep Purple* showed a band taking the first move in the direction which they would perfect some time later. In this regard, their early work mirrors that of Yes, for example, whose first two albums likewise saw them hinting, albeit extremely well, at the template they would go on to make their own.

Album Cover.

The album cover photograph is fairly typical of the time, with the band appearing rather stiffly in fashionable outfits purchased for them at the notable London boutique the 'Mr Fish Emporium', where they did the photo shoot.

Incidentally, and possibly of coincidental naming, the owner and fashion designer Michael Fish was the man behind the infamous 'kipper tie'! The same shot was used for both the American and British covers, but in different formats; while the US version had the shot repeated several times in squares on the front cover, both colour and monochrome, the UK release went for a much simpler design, with the one big shot for the whole cover, against a purple background (naturally) with the title above. The band name was omitted from the UK cover, whereas in the American design it was highlighted in a different colour in order to emphasise it.

'And The Address'. (Blackmore, Lord)

The first track on the album was also the first piece written by Blackmore and Lord – before the group had formed around them, in fact – and also the first track to be recorded on the initial day in the studio (Hey Joe, Hush and Help were the others to be completed on that first day). Interestingly, and somewhat amusingly, Nick Simper has claimed (in an interview with Purple devotee and author Jerry Bloom) that the unusual title comes from an exclamation made 'after a gentleman had broken wind' ('...and the address...'), but this is unsubstantiated. An instrumental, it is in fact an extremely effective way to kick off the album, with a minute or so of free-form organ fading in gradually only to give way to a series of dramatic power chords introducing Blackmore's guitar carrying the melody. The sound is very much of its time, in a slightly psychedelic, 'proto-prog' way, but moves along at an energetic tempo, introducing Lord and Blackmore as the clear musical leaders via some fairly impressive soloing. The track was used to open all of their shows up until the release of the next album, but was somewhat disappointingly dropped thereafter. Deep Purple had made their presence felt, though it would take some time for their homeland to join the party...

'Hush'. (South)

It is quite an unusual phenomenon for a cover version to effectively launch a band's career single-handedly, not to mention defining them, in the American market at least, for some time, but *Hush* did that in spectacular fashion for Deep Purple. Released as a single in July 1968, it reached number 4 in the US chart and number 2 in Canada, despite making barely a ripple in the UK. The success of the single more or less dragged the album up with it to become a sizeable American hit (peaking at 24), and to this day there are many fans in the US who cite this first line-up as their favourite Purple era. The track was originally written by Joe South – based partly on a traditional Gospel song – and first recorded by Billy Joe Royal in 1967, for whom it became a minor hit. The Purple recording follows the arrangement of the Royal version quite faithfully, although much more dramatically. Opening with a slightly incongruous crashing intro, it gives way to Lord's churning, funky organ underpinning Blackmore's fiery lead lines. Evans delivers the song well, though it is somewhat amusing to hear this Eton-born, very English singer delivering the line 'I can't eat, y'all, and I can't sleep'! A hilarious promo film was made of the band clearly debunking the whole lip-synching culture as they looned about in an open air poolside location, complete with large open fire. Evans sings alternately in swimming trunks and towel and lounging in a deckchair, while Lord, clad in black leather trenchcoat, attacks such 'instruments' as garden furniture and a fishing net, with which he rescues a stricken Evans from the pool. Simper, meanwhile, temporarily abandons his bass to run around with a tiny wheelbarrow. Showing an early example of the band's oft-demonstrated sense of humour, it is well worth seeking out online.

'One More Rainy Day'. (Lord, Evans)

An original composition by Lord and Evans, and the B-Side of the 'Hush' single, this was the final song to be recorded for the album, on the third day in the studio. Opening with the sound of thundery weather (taken from a BBC sound effects record, as were all of the similar bridging elements between songs on the album), Lord's organ leads us into the song in strident fashion, but it soon settles into a pleasant if unremarkable song, treading the slightly psychedelic pop road which was infested with identikit would-be pop stars in those late-'60s days. It's a mildly diverting song to listen to, but far from a classic – and certainly a long way from being representative of where Purple would travel later.

'Prelude: Happiness / I'm So Glad'. (Blackmore, Evans, Lord, Paice, Simper / James)

A two-part piece here, as the band preface a cover of the Skip James song 'I'm So Glad', popularised by Cream shortly beforehand, with an instrumental introduction of their own. Titled 'Prelude: Happiness', and taking up almost three minutes of the seven and a half minute track, this is actually the more interesting section of the medley by some distance. Clearly the brainchild of Lord – despite the somewhat unlikely credit to all five members, including Evans – it is a dextrous keyboard-led workout, incorporating themes from the Rimsky-Korsakov work *Scheherazade*. Indeed, it proves something of an anti-climax when the band transition into a somewhat uninspired arrangement of 'I'm So Glad'. Once again, there is some nice organ work from Lord, and brief flashes from Blackmore, but it becomes very repetitive, with Evans' decidedly non-joyful intonation not helping matters. Clearly, the band already had some aptitude for stretching themselves beyond conventional 'pop' songwriting limits, and an extended version of the prelude would arguably have constituted a stronger track. In fact,' I'm So Glad' was suggested by Evans and Paice, who had played it in their previous band The Maze, but the timing of the recording so soon after Cream's version brought it into the public eye made it appear somewhat unimaginative.

'Mandrake Root'. (Blackmore, Lord, Evans)

The opening track on the second side of the album is another which was intended to be an instrumental, but rather than have two instrumental tracks on the album, along with 'Prelude: Happiness', some cursory (and mildly suggestive) lyrics were added by Evans before the recording. The track takes its name from the hallucinatory plant, which was said to scream when pulled from the ground, but it is more directly taken from the name of a band which Blackmore was in the process of forming prior to the Roundabout offer coming his way. The origin of the song is somewhat controversial, as there are two schools of thought as to its writing. Officially, it was written by Blackmore and Lord around the time of the band's formation, but there were claims by a man named Bill Parkinson, a guitarist who had played, like Blackmore, in The Savages, that the track was taken directly from a piece he wrote called 'Lost Soul'. It was later rumoured that the band had settled with him for a fairly modest sum. However, the other version of events is that Blackmore wrote the piece heavily influenced by Jimi Hendrix, which is backed up by the fact that the main riff bears a strong resemblance to the latter's hit 'Foxy Lady'. Whatever the truth of the matter, it was a strong piece, and a natural vehicle for soloing, which was borne out by its long life in the Purple set as a lengthy springboard for improvisation. Unquestionably the track which showcases the band's instrumental prowess and virtuoso soloing ability most obviously on the album (Lord and Blackmore are backed up by Paice's frenzied drumming to produce an aural chaos similar to the live freak-outs Pink Floyd were doing at the time), nevertheless the studio version's six-minute duration was still only the starting point, with live versions regularly lasting for well over 20 minutes.

'Help'. (Lennon, McCartney)

Back to the cover versions again here, for this imaginative adaptation of the Beatles classic. Owing a lot to the template laid down by Vanilla Fudge – an early favourite of the band – the song is slowed down to a virtual crawl, with every ounce of drama wrung out of it in Evans' impassioned vocal. In truth, this is a very creditable and effective rendition, not least because it follows the brief which John Lennon had in mind when he wrote the song; as he has gone on record as saying that he wrote it as a slow song, but that the tempo was sped up significantly in order to make it more commercial. In that sense, the Purple version can be seen as the first attempt to perform the song in the way that it was intended, and indeed it does bring out the desperate sentiment in the lyric more than the much lighter Beatles recording. Without doubt one of the strongest tracks on the album, and one for which Evans' smooth, 'crooner' type voice was actually ideally suited.

'Love Help Me'. (Blackmore, Evans)

This Blackmore / Evans composition is another fairly unremarkable original song, beginning with more of those slightly tiresome sound effects before a grandiose set of power chords introduce the band playing with some energy and aggression, but unfortunately not all that much in the way of substance. There are some ill-advised vocal harmony sections which call to mind a half-hearted Beach Boys track, while Evans himself tries manfully but fails to stamp his authority on the vocal. Blackmore solos all over the cut, seemingly trying to lift it above the mundane but, again, it is far from his best work. Interestingly, he uses the wah-wah pedal extensively on the track – something he would do only occasionally for the band going forward – and it doesn't really suit his style, as he sounds like a man trying a little too hard. Probably the weakest track on the album, it showed that the band were yet to properly develop their compositional abilities.

'Hey Joe'. (Roberts)

Another fairly unimaginative choice of cover, given the success that Hendrix had enjoyed with the song and also the fact that groups up and down the country were including the song as a regular in their live sets at the time. Still, the arrangement is interesting, without a doubt. The lengthy introduction illustrates Lord's classical influence again, as the band 'borrow' liberally from 'The Miller's Dance', from the 1919 ballet *The Three Cornered Hat*, by Spanish composer Manuel de Falla. This is set against a staccato rhythm strikingly similar to that which would make an appearance a couple of years down the road on 'Child In Time', and it takes until almost two and a half minutes in for the song proper to begin. At just over four minutes in, Lord's strident organ ushers in a reprise of the opening section before Blackmore comes in with a guitar solo which, though excellent, is very reminiscent of the classic Hendrix rendition. After another verse and chorus, another small helping of that 'Child In Time' rhythm pattern sets us up for a big, album-closing, series of power chords, which are followed by the somewhat incongruous sound of footsteps and a door closing. It's an entertaining seven minutes for sure, and closes the album quite strongly, but in the final analysis less than half of the duration has any connection with the original song – which was written by US songwriter Billy Roberts in 1972, although on early pressings it was mistakenly credited to the members of Purple themselves. Poor old Manuel de Falla never got a look in, of course!

Related Song.

'Shadows'. (Lord, Evans, Simper, Blackmore)

When the band recorded the demo tape which led to the album, the only track thus recorded which failed to make the cut for the final album was this one – and it's something of a shame as the song does have promise. Driven along by a strident, marching verse riff, it has the ability to lodge in the listener's brain after only a single listen, and is pleasingly infectious. The chorus, with a melody not entirely dissimilar to the Monkees' 'Daydream Believer', is less riveting, but it's brief, and we're soon back that great propulsive main riff once again. Blackmore again uses the wah-wah here, but in more successful fashion than on 'Love Help Me', and the guitar work is more confident and fluid overall than that track. It certainly could be argued that the inclusion of 'Shadows' could well have strengthened the album overall, but at least it finally surfaced some decades later as a bonus track on a CD re-release of the album.

The Book Of Taliesyn

Personnel:
Rod Evans: vocals
Ritchie Blackmore: guitars
Jon Lord: keyboards
Nick Simper: bass guitar
Ian Paice: drums and percussion
Record Label: Harvest (UK), Tetragrammaton (US)
Recorded August and October 1968, produced by Derek Lawrence.
UK release date: June 1969. US release date: October 1968.
Highest chart places: UK: Did not chart, USA: 54
Running time: 43:57

Album facts.

Appearing an astonishing three months after the debut in America, where it
was rushed out to capitalise on an Autumn tour, the album was held over a
significant length of time in the UK, eventually getting a release in June 1969,
when the band were doing a tour of their home country. Absurdly, by this
time, the band had recorded AND released their third album in the US, and
were already toying with line-up changes. Recorded at De Lane Lea studios
in London, the UK release was, notably, the first album put out on EMI's new
'progressive' Harvest label, but it still failed to trouble the chart compilers
in any way, as opposed to the US where is hit a rather modest 54. The title
of the album is something of an oddity, coming from the 14th century Welsh
manuscript *The Book of Taliesin*, but altering the spelling of the final word.
The sleeve notes to the original US release of the album continue this quasi-
mystical approach, referencing a bard of King Arthur's court, Taliesyn, as a
spiritual guide, taking the listener on an exploration of the band's personalities
and souls. All of which is fairly hard to stack up against a cover of 'River Deep
Mountain High', it has to be said.

Album cover.

The cover artwork was a big progression from the debut, as band and record
company seemed to grasp the value of appealing to the new 'hippy' audience.
Carnaby Street suits and bouffant hairdos were no longer the way to go, and
the brief this time was to go much further out on a limb. The cover was a
gatefold, for a start, with suitably *de rigeur* fantasy artwork by future university
professor, John Vernon Lord. In fact, this was the only album cover that he ever
worked on, as he moved into teaching and book illustration shortly thereafter,
but he recalls getting a brief to produce something with an 'Arthurian /
fantasy touch', and to illustrate the title and band members' names by hand
(indeed, the latter appear somewhat incongruously adorning the side of what
resembles some kind of hot air balloon). The album title and band name

actually appear three times within the painting, in a progressively smaller size, where they battle for space with assorted castles, minstrels, chess pieces and various animals. It is quite eccentric to say the least, but oddly fascinating. The remainder of the cover – rear and inner gatefold – was disappointingly earthbound in nature, with monochrome photos of the band abounding, and with the unbearably pretentious sleeve notes being replaced in the UK by a photo of the band around a grand piano.

'Listen, Learn, Read On'. (Blackmore, Evans, Lord, Paice)

Credited to the full band minus Simper, and cut from very much the same cloth as 'And The Address' from the debut album, this proggy-psychedelic piece is in some respects a sort of 'unofficial title track', as it contains the chorus line 'You've got to turn the pages, read the Book Of Taliesyn'. In fact, the song takes its inspiration from the cover painting as, contained within its lyrics, are references to such elements of that design as the hare, the chessmen, the minstrels, the castles and even, indirectly, the fish (via the unlikely line 'I shall be of more service to thee than three hundred salmon')! The outstanding contributor here is without a doubt Ian Paice, whose frantic drumming keeps the track in top gear and instils a sense of urgency which keeps it just the right side of ridicule – which is no mean feat, given the way Evans solemnly intones the verses in heavily echoed spoken-word fashion as if delivering words of great import and power. Away from this somewhat absurd affectation, and as Paice thrashes away, Blackmore steps up to deliver a heavily distorted solo which is far from his best, both in tone and execution. It's an enjoyably over-the-top romp in its way, but it does give the impression that the album is going to be some sort of conceptual affair, with this as its 'overture' of sorts, as it climaxes with the line '…and what hereafter will occur'. Sadly that was not to be the case, as what did occur immediately thereafter was an instrumental followed by a distinctly non-mystical Neil Diamond cover…

'Wring That Neck'. (Blackmore, Lord, Simper, Paice)

Another instrumental here, credited to the band except for Evans, and one which proved to be a regular in the band's set for years to come. Beginning with Lord's opening salvo (sounding oddly like the Woody Woodpecker laugh I might add), followed by some massively booming drum beats, this track fairly rips along from start to finish, with only a short, unaccompanied Blackmore part at around four minutes to throw the returning theme into dramatically sharpened relief. Lord is on top form here, while Blackmore appears to have his heart in things much more than on the opening track – indeed, his solo gives the biggest pointer thus far to his signature style which would be developed over the coming years. The title, of course, could just as easily refer to the neck of a guitar as to any act of violence, but this did not stop Warners in America getting decidedly cold feet about it, and it was renamed as the seemingly random 'Hard Road' on early US pressings. The track would go on to carve another small niche in the world of rock trivia not too far in the future, which we will look at when discussing *Deep Purple In Rock*, in 1970...

'Kentucky Woman'. (Diamond)

Once again we see a cover version making its way onto the record (the first of three, in fact), though given the fact that the album was recorded only three months after the debut we should perhaps not be surprised that original material might have been a little thin on the ground at the time. On this occasion, it is a song from the somewhat unlikely pen of Neil Diamond, though it is certainly one of his more upbeat compositions. The Purple version retains the vocal melody and the basis of the song, but takes it in a rockier direction, away from the acoustic-based arrangement on Diamond's 1967 original. It's entertaining but for the most part unremarkable, with Blackmore again sounding as if he is soloing in his sleep, with only Lord's typically-wild keyboard solo taking the excitement level up a notch. It's a more complete arrangement than the original for sure, but the area where it falls badly short is in Evans' vocal, which is delivered without any semblance of the soul which oozes from the Neil Diamond version, and another sign that the band really did need someone stronger fronting them. The track was released as a single, in slightly edited form, but did not chart as high as 'Hush' in the States. In the UK, of course, it sank without trace. The B-Side was 'Wring That Neck', which one imagines must have come as a shock to some of the pop-oriented teens who purchased the single!

'Exposition / We Can Work It Out'. (Blackmore, Simper, Lord, Paice / Lennon, McCartney)

Yes, it's that 'cover version' trail again, with the Beatles the target for the second album on the run, but this is in the two-part style of 'I'm So Glad' from the debut album, as the somewhat pretentiously titled opening instrumental 'Exposition' runs to almost three of the seven minutes here. Once again the classically-trained Lord is raiding his bag of orchestral influences, this time with Beethoven (an obvious rearrangement of part of his *Seventh Symphony*) and Tchaikovsky (a lesser, but still present, bit of *Romeo And Juliet*) being the 'borrowings' of choice. It's still a very entertaining and superbly played introduction, but a little nod to those great composers alongside the names of the Purple members (minus Evans again) would have been a nice admission. Interestingly, it seems odd that Lord gets so little recognition for his 'rocking the classics' on these early albums, while his keyboard contemporary Keith Emerson would be celebrated for doing very much the same thing at very much the same time. The Beatles section of the track is far less interesting, being driven by Blackmore's insistent guitar licks throughout, trying another bit of the old Vanilla Fudge trick by slowing down the mid-section, but generally ending up as one of the less remarkable Beatles interpretations of the '60s. It's certainly nowhere near as impressive or inventive as 'Help', with Evans once again sounding as if he is reading the weather forecast rather than pouring out his soul to his partner as they try to salvage their relationship.

'Shield'. (Blackmore, Evans, Lord)

Opening the second side of the vinyl, this Blackmore / Evans / Lord original is just about as trippy as Deep Purple ever got. Opening with an insistent bass figure, it settles into a mellow groove similar to Cream's more psychedelic moments, and underpinned by some mantra-like percussion from Paice, particularly during the guitar solo which takes us into the 'acid rock' realm typical of the times. Blackmore is clearly out of his comfort zone, but he manages to sprinkle some magic over proceedings as the track gently marinates in a stew of rippling piano and insistent bass. The lyrics are steeped in mystical imagery involving children playing on a green hill, fathers smoking 'the pipe of a better life' and the hoped-for protection of a nebulous shield of some sort. It probably symbolises the desire to cling to a safe, harmonious family life, but it works well in its fantastical finery when put together with the music.

'Anthem'. (Lord, Evans)

A rare Lord / Evans composition is up next, in the shape of the stately ballad 'Anthem'. Evans' lyric is a fairly standard take on the old 'guy misses girl, finds the night time the hardest' template, but it's quite well written for what it is, and on this occasion he evokes some emotion in his delivery, as Lord's beautiful melody is clearly the perfect vehicle for his voice. The vocal harmonies in the chorus threaten to over-egg the pudding somewhat, but it is, for all that, a very good song. Where it takes off to another level, however, comes after three minutes or so when the instrumental section kicks in. Lord's solo organ passage brings things right down, before being accompanied by his own sensitively arranged string quartet. Blackmore is next to enter the fray with a delicate guitar solo, which is made fascinating when you realise he is playing in the exact style of a violin soloing over a quartet, yet with a pick. Very, very clever. The band come back in at that point to usher in a further Blackmore solo passage over the fuller sound, bringing an almost tangible sense of relief after the deliberately restrained preceding section. Evans returns to deliver the final verse and chorus before the song comes to an end, with that lengthy instrumental section standing as a minor masterclass of subtlety and arrangement skill. Along with 'Wring That Neck', certainly the outstanding piece on the album. Notably, due to its complexity and string arrangement, this was one of two songs from the album never played live (the other being 'Exposition / We Can Work It Out').

'River Deep Mountain High'. (Barry, Greenwich, Spector)

Well, what can we say, as we reach the end of the album with a ten minute version of the Ike And Tina Turner classic? Well, we could certainly say things like 'overblown' and 'filler', but let's take a look at the track. Firstly, of course, it isn't ten minutes of 'River Deep Mountain High' at all, but another example of the lengthy unrelated intro so beloved of the band, and Lord in particular, on this album. This time out, there isn't even a separately titled opening, with band writing credits, despite the fact that the song itself doesn't enter proceedings until four and a half minutes in, and even then the next 40 seconds or so are taken up by Evans' slow, solemn intoning of the first two lines of the song, like a sort of '60s hipster monk. So, by the time they get going, half of the track is the titular song itself. It's hard to see why the intro is left without separate credit, although it may be simply because there is very, very little in the way of an actual tune buried in there. Instead, the band flail around for four and a half minutes like a fly unable to find a surface on which to settle, with Lord up to his classical borrowing antics again as he is unable to resist slipping in a little *Also Sprach Zarathustra* in there. This is not wholly unsurprising as it had been made rather popular by its use in the film *2001: A Space Odyssey* earlier in the year and it would become even more ubiquitous the following year as the music chosen to accompany TV coverage of the Apollo XI moon landing. This time out he can hardly be accused of theft, however, as he doesn't even claim a credit for himself anyway.

Leaving that lumbering beast of an introduction aside, how do the band approach the song? Well, the answer would be best described as 'competently but unexceptionally', with only Paice's drum work generating much in the way of excitement. It follows the original more or less, although differing in key ways. We don't get the Phil Spector 'Wall Of Sound' arrangement so familiar from the original, but we do get an overwrought Evans performance bordering on histrionics. His wild-eyed cry of 'It gets higher! So higher!!' evokes nothing so much as Spinal Tap having a crack at the song. Amazingly, an edited version of this was released as a single in the US and Canada. Sliced down mercilessly to less than three minutes, it actually makes more sense without the extra baggage, and this slightly more focused edit made it to just outside the US Top 50 ('Listen, Learn, Read On' was on the flip side). In a sense, it is an appropriate way to close an album which has its moments, but is over-ambitious and lacking in quality original material. It sounds exactly like what it is – namely, a band being pressured into the studio and told 'you have fifteen minutes of good songs? Great, make us an album'. This sort of crazy schedule would not let up for some time to come, unfortunately...

Related Songs.

'Playground.' (Blackmore, Simper, Lord, Paice)
A band-composed instrumental out-take, this would actually have made a reasonable addition to the album. Certainly it could have replaced the lengthy and largely pointless introduction to 'River Deep Mountain High' without weakening things in any way. A nimble bass line from Simper underscores

proceedings while Blackmore and Lord lay the main course over the top. In fact, the main riff to this track possesses a notable similarity to 'Rat Bat Blue', from 1973's *Who Do We Think We Are* album, so it may be that it was filed away for possible future use back in 1968, as opposed to being discarded entirely. It has been suggested that there might have been lyrics intended for this which were never written, and this is a feasible idea since there is not quite enough variety going on to fully convince as a purely instrumental track. As for the title, it may well be that it was a reference back to the Roundabout name, but that is personal speculation. The track eventually surfaced some decades later as a CD bonus track, so it belatedly had its moment in the sun...

'Oh No No No' (Berns, Leander)

Another studio outtake, this is a cover of a song by the prolific '60s songwriter Bert Berns. Not as familiar a name as he perhaps should be, Berns was responsible for a string of hits from 'Under The Boardwalk' to 'Piece Of My Heart', before his untimely death at 38 in 1967. This, however, is not one of his better known works, and is a fairly unremarkable pop song, not especially well suited to the Purple treatment. This version starts off promisingly, with an excellent Blackmore lead line over the introductory bars, but once the song begins in earnest, that promise begins to dissipate. The track is another which ultimately made it onto the album as a CD bonus track, but it was an understandable decision to leave it off in the first place.

'It's All Over.' (Berns, Leander)

Another Berns song, this was one of three tracks recorded around this time for a *BBC Top Gear* session broadcast in January 1969. An odd choice of song to attempt, it's a slow blues previously recorded by Ben E King a few years previously, and though the Purple version slots in more contemporary psychedelic fairy-dust, it doesn't really rise above that into anything special. Blackmore solos all over it, including an introductory passage which lasts over a minute, but his tone is thin and the track is weak.

'Hey Bop A Re Bop.' (Blackmore, Evans, Lord, Paice)

The second song from that same BBC session, this has to be better than its title, right? Wrong. Musically, this is simply a dry run for 'The Painter' from the following album, in very tentative form, while lyrically it is hopeless. Evans sounds as if he is making up the lyrics (about meeting someone named Gloria at the station) on the spot, and they have no connection whatsoever with the strange title, which appears to be plucked from the Lionel Hampton jazz composition 'Hey Ba Ba Re Bop' for no fathomable reason. A bizarre yet forgettable exercise. Whatever prompted this to be recorded for a prestigious BBC session can only be imagined. Happily, the third song recorded for that session was a version of 'Wring That Neck', so all was not lost.

Deep Purple

Personnel:
Rod Evans: vocals
Ritchie Blackmore: guitars
Jon Lord: keyboards
Nick Simper: bass guitar
Ian Paice: drums and percussion
Record Label: Harvest (UK), Tetragrammaton (US)
Recorded January – March 1969, Produced by Derek Lawrence.
UK release date: September 1969. US release date: June 1969.
Highest chart places: UK: Did not chart, USA: 162
Running time: 44:34

Album facts.

To say that this album had a complex gestation and release period would be to severely understate proceedings. Undertaken between January and March 1969, recording sessions at De Lane Lea were conducted around a substantial UK tour at the same time – the final (unsuccessful) attempt by this line-up to gain any significant traction at home. By the time the album came out in the US, in June, the previous album was only just being released in the UK and, to make the waters even more muddy, Ian Gillan and Roger Glover were already being lined up to replace Evans and Simper. When the album came out in the UK, in September, not only was this new line-up already in place, but they were already recording Lord's *Concerto For Group And Orchestra* at the Royal Albert Hall! It is hardly surprising that the album 'fell through the cracks', so to speak, not only failing to register in the UK again, but also limping to a massively disappointing 162 in the US. In hindsight, the album's reputation has grown over the years, and it is often looked back on as the most musically successful recording by the Mk I version of the band. As with the previous two releases, it was produced by Derek Lawrence, but it would be the last one he would work on.

Album cover.

The stark, dramatic illustration on the album cover was a detail of one of the panels from Hieronymus Bosch's triptych painting *The Garden Of Earthly Delights*, dating from around 1599, depicting Hell, or The last Judgement. Another section of this same panel had been used for a cover design a couple of years previously by the experimental psychedelic folk band Pearls Before Swine, on their album *One Nation Underground*. While the original painting is, of course, in colour, the album cover appeared in monochrome; this was actually due to an error on the part of US label Tetragrammaton for the first pressing, after which the band elected to leave it that way. One interesting feature of the cover was that the gatefold opened vertically rather than horizontally, to depict the painting the correct way up, which is an unusual, though not unique, instance among vinyl album covers. It's not all Bosch, however, as a closer look at the right side of the front cover reveals the band themselves, nestling beneath a naked man being crucified on a giant harp, and in front of what are presumably a group of damned souls. They've probably played worse venues. The unsettling nature of the painting led many record shops, particularly in the US, refuse to stock it, or at least decline to display it prominently. Inside the gatefold, meanwhile, was a complete contrast to this stark monochrome – at least in the UK – as the album opened to display two panels of the brightest day-glo pink (or if we are being charitable, 'purple') colour one could imagine. It was eye-catching if nothing else, however, though oddly enough the left hand panel was otherwise blank, with notes about the tracks all appearing on the right side in black lettering. Across the Atlantic in Canada things were a little more toned down, with a photo of the band accompanying advertisements for the previous albums...

'Chasing Shadows'. (Paice, Lord)

An insistent, tribal percussion rhythm from Ian Paice opens this song, and continues right through it (accompanied by a sinuous bassline from Simper). Co-written by Paice along with Jon Lord, the song is – according to the album notes – 'about one of Jon's nightmares', which explains his lyric writing here. Paice is the driving force behind the piece, establishing a bedrock of insistent, repetitive drumming which was augmented later by overdubs of other percussion instruments such as cowbell, timbales and maracas, while Lord and Blackmore provide regular slashing power chords, emphasising the beat still further. It possesses a dynamism almost wholly lacking from the previous two albums, and shows a band striving beyond the dated psychedelia which had permeated those earlier efforts. Blackmore contributes some stinging lead guitar – again utilising the wah-wah pedal – which shows him growing in confidence and maturity before our eyes (or ears). The uneasy feel generated by the surreal imagery of Lord's lyrics only adds to the effect (and makes the listener glad not to have been experiencing the nightmare in question!), and it is something of a shame that the song was performed live rarely, if ever.

'Blind'. (Lord)

Once again we see Lord contributing the lyrics here, as this track is written entirely by him. To great effect, as it happens, because this is a tremendous song, both lyrically and musically, and the sleeve note description of it being 'a love song, sort of squeezed into the format of a 12-bar blues' goes nowhere near doing it justice. Lyrically obtuse and evocative, it deals with the subject of loneliness and abandonment from the point of view of the changing seasons, and this downbeat yet beautiful mood is matched by the stately feel of the music. Embroidered throughout by Lord's adept harpsichord fills (surely one of the more unusual instruments to take a leading role on a rock song), its

23

descending, minor key feel is similar to Cream on tracks such as 'White Room' or 'Tales Of Brave Ulysses'. Blackmore's stinging solo here is one of his best up to this point, heavily distorted and distilled to perfection, with another use of that wah-wah pedal judged nicely on this occasion. In all, 'Blind' is one of the most underrated songs in the whole Deep Purple catalogue, being as it is a lesser known track on one of the lesser known albums, and a joyous discovery for those who chance upon it.

'Lalena'. (Leitch)

The only cover song on the album, this track was a relatively minor hit for its composer, Donovan, in 1968. According to the songwriter himself, it was inspired by the Austrian singer/actress (and wife of composer Kurt Weill) Lotte Lenya, and in particular her character in the 1931 film version of Brecht/Weill's *The Threepenny Opera*. An achingly sad song, the arrangement here is exceptionally well done. Coming in two minutes longer than the sparse acoustic guitar and vocal of the original, everything here is sympathetically added to the mix, with no temptation to blur things with an overblown band arrangement. Sparse notes are sporadically dropped into the backing like raindrops into water, pre-empting the similar effect in the opening section of Mike Oldfield's *Tubular Bells* by some four years, while the brief forays into near-grandiosity by the band imbue the melody with a hint of King Crimson's 'Epitaph' – released later the same year – in places. The growth of the band by this point is quite remarkable, and all the more ironic given the fact that by the time it was heard, it was an echo from a band which no longer existed...

'Fault Line'. (Blackmore, Simper, Lord, Paice) / 'The Painter.' (Blackmore, Simper, Evans, Lord, Paice)

Another 'song with an instrumental intro' trick here – albeit this time an original rather than a cover version, expanded. The short (under two minutes) 'Fault Line' is an experimental piece, consisting mainly of Blackmore's meandering guitar over an eerily repetitive background of drums and organ played backward. As a sort of sound collage, it holds some interest, but is not essential by any means. According to the album notes, it was inspired by the band discovering they were going to be in Los Angeles 'at earthquake time', although the idea that there is some sort of 'earthquake season' in the same way as the 'hurricane season' does seem slightly odd. 'The Painter' is, as previously noted, roughly the same music as the radio session track 'Hey Bop A Re Bop', although significantly better this time out. The title may give the impression that this track is going to be reflective and introspective, musing on the life and artistic calling of the titular painter, but it is actually a quite simple and upbeat lyric, calling on the painter to 'colour up my life', a writer to 'write me up a play' and a singer to 'let me sing a song', all of which are presumably to make the world a happier place. It's well enough delivered by Evans, while Blackmore and Lord's solos are both exemplary. A sharp, focused and very good track to end a strong side of vinyl.

'Why Didn't Rosemary'. (Blackmore, Evans, Simper, Lord, Paice)
This full band composition is one which could easily be misunderstood with a cursory listen, as the hook lyric 'Why didn't Rosemary ever take the pill' would appear to point to the singer bemoaning an unplanned pregnancy, but the truth is somewhat more interesting. The band had been to the cinema to watch the Roman Polanski horror film *Rosemary's Baby*, in which housewife Rosemary (Mia Farrow) is impregnated by the devil himself, leading to all manner of troubles with the ensuing demonic offspring, and they returned suitably inspired to write this somewhat tongue in cheek song about the whole devil-impregnation scenario. In actual fact, if the suggestion about taking the pill had been followed, the film would probably have been significantly shorter! Musically, the track follows a loose upbeat blues format: 'loose' because, as the liner notes state, it progressed beyond the usual 12 bar format, as the verses have 14 bars and the guitar solo verses have 17! It is also claimed to be loosely based on a song by American blues pianist Otis Spann, but there is no clue given as to what song that may be. Once again, Lord and Blackmore both contribute a solo, but Lord's is fairly short while Blackmore, following up, takes centre stage for quite a lengthy, yet well worked out, display. Overall, while it might not win any awards for profound insight or originality (unless of course you count the feat of fitting 17 bars into a 12-bar tune), it is nevertheless an entertaining track which appears to show the band loosening up and enjoying themselves.

'Bird Has Flown'. (Blackmore, Evans, Lord)
A heavy psychedelic rock feel to this track is provided by the insistent, driving guitar riff powering it along, finding Blackmore gleefully seizing the wah-wah opportunity again, only this time not just to embellish a solo but to underpin the whole song. The track is actually an extended variant on an earlier B-Side called 'The Bird Has Flown' (see below), and it is a very successful, memorable rocker – developing into a powerful and inventive instrumental coda driven first by Blackmore's guitar solo, then some unaccompanied Lord emoting gravely on the Hammond organ, and finally seen out by some great ensemble playing. It does, however, underline the fact that Rod Evans simply had to go. While he manages okay in the verses, where he just has to follow the riff for the vocal melody, there is a mid-section of the song which finds him crooning in an embarrassingly 'cabaret' form, entirely at odds with the track and indeed the band in general. He could sing, without doubt, but he couldn't sing with Deep Purple, that much was by now decided. Written by the Blackmore/ Lord partnership, the song carries a somewhat bizarre message about the nature of comparative emotional suffering, as it dismisses the problems faced by a beggar, a lonely hermit in a cave and some unidentified children in a 'distant house', which we fear may be orphans. Indeed, the life issues faced by these unfortunates are waved away when compared to the anguish felt by the unfortunate lover whose 'bird has flown'. So the message is, if you're

penniless, without any human companionship or indeed parents, cheer up because at least you haven't had a break-up with someone. There may be disagreement on the streets of India about this, for example, but we'll let it slide. A good track for all of this lyrical nonsense.

'April'. (Blackmore, Lord)

The closing track on the album is also the longest studio track ever recorded by the band, in any incarnation. A truly expansive progressive rock exercise, it opens with a four minute instrumental section of the highest quality, with Blackmore first accompanying Lord on acoustic guitar, before he straps on the electric and the pair begin trading solos in familiar yet excellent fashion. At the four and a half minute mark, the track takes a stylistic shift into four minutes of pure classical music, as a troupe of orchestral musicians troop in to perform a section of pure Jon Lord bravura. For the final third of the song, the band power back in, with the drums this time heavily in the mix, as Evans enters the fray with some rather depressing musings on the cruelty of the tragic month of April (we do not learn why), accompanied by declamations of grey skies where there should be blue, etc. It's quite fitting as a closer to what is undoubtedly the most melancholic – and at times downright miserable – album in the Purple catalogue, and yet curiously effective and enjoyable for all that. A Blackmore / Lord composition, it was initially brought to the table by the guitarist already titled, whereupon Lord got his classical hooks into perfecting it, including dropping in the orchestral section fully formed. The sleeve notes merely refer to it being about the month of April, which is 'sad, to us'(again we do not know why this should be), but more prosaically April is Blackmore's birth month, and his then-wife Babs has said (to Jerry Bloom) that she and Ritchie met in April and that the song was titled for that meeting. If that is so, then we must assume that the catastrophic sadness which is continually bemoaned by the band is so much artistic license, and an exercise in introspective misery. Still, who doesn't enjoy a bit of that now and again? Anyhow, with this track both the album and the recording career of Deep Purple Mk I were over.

Related songs.

'Emmaretta'. (Blackmore, Evans, Lord)

A fairly basic three-minute riff-driven effort, 'Emmaretta' was recorded in January 1969, specifically written with the intention of being a single, and released as such ahead of the album, as a 'teaser' of sorts. That it failed to make the cut for the album itself is not particularly unsurprising, as it is fairly undistinguished compared to most of the album material, and indeed failed to incite any noticeable excitement among singles buyers either. Blackmore features most heavily here, contributing a quite nice choppy riff straight out of the Hendrix playbook to anchor the song and underscore the verses.

With some use of that wah-wah pedal again (also featured on the somewhat unremarkable guitar solo), it's the best part of the track without doubt. The title was inspired by Emmaretta Marks, a cast member of the popular 'hippie musical' of the time, *Hair*, whom Evans had met and been impressed by, but it must be said that his lyric to this song is banal in the extreme. The opening salvo of 'Emmaretta / Did you get my letter? / I sent it to you' seems faintly absurd, as the question would have been an odd one indeed if he had sent it to someone else. Later, in the less than memorable section which might be referred to as the chorus, he becomes moved to rhyme 'Need you child' with 'Drives me wild', and even manages to cram 'A thousand miles' in there. Other than Blackmore's riff, it's not a song to rate highly in the Deep Purple annals, and Jon Lord's songwriting credit seems a little surprising.

'The Bird Has Flown'. (Blackmore, Evans, Lord)

The B-Side to the US pressing of 'Emmaretta' (the UK got 'Wring That Neck' yet again), this is actually the original recorded version of the album track 'Bird Has Flown', with the definite article added to the title by way of differentiation. It is worth treating this as a different piece, as it is taken at a faster pace and played noticeably heavier. Shorn of the excellent climactic session on the album version, it is certainly the lesser version of the two, but it works well as a more focused commercial piece, and in many ways would have made a better A side than 'Emmaretta'. Blackmore's slightly 'eastern' sounding guitar line behind Evans' 'cabaret' chorus is much higher in the mix here, and improves that section, as well as pointing the way for some of the guitarist's future influences.

Concerto For Group And Orchestra

Personnel:
Ian Gillan: vocals
Ritchie Blackmore: guitars
Jon Lord: keyboards
Roger Glover: bass guitar
Ian Paice: drums and percussion
The Royal Philharmonic Orchestra (conducted by Malcolm Arnold)
Record Label: Harvest (UK), Tetragrammaton (US)
Recorded 24 September 1969, produced by Deep Purple.
UK release date: January 1970. US release date: December 1969.
Highest chart places: UK: 26, USA: Did Not Chart
Running time: 59:26

Album facts.

A very odd album with which to usher in the Mk II line-up of the band, but so be it. The idea for this pet project of Jon Lord's was born from him happening to listen to a 1961 album called *Bernstein Plays Brubeck Plays Bernstein*, a convoluted title for a recording of jazz musician Dave Brubeck's quartet playing with the New York Philharmonic Orchestra, conducted by *West Side Story* composer Leonard Bernstein. The idea appealed to Lord's restless musical soul, and it planted the seed of the idea about a rock band doing the same thing. He mentioned the idea to Purple's then management team of Tony Edwards and John Coletta and requested that plans were put underway. He was somewhat taken aback by the announcement shortly afterward that the Royal Albert Hall had been booked for a performance of the yet to be composed work, but it did serve to focus his mind! He continued to work on the score at the same time as recording sessions for the next 'regular' album *Deep Purple In Rock* were ongoing, which led to a massive workload at the time. He was helped enormously by Malcolm Arnold, who had agreed to conduct the orchestra during the performance, and the completed score was duly delivered on time for rehearsals to take place. Some members of the band were vehemently opposed to the project (Blackmore in particular, but also new vocalist Ian Gillan), as they feared that it might set a precedent for that sort of work, and detract from the band's rock ambitions. Roger Glover was more pragmatic, stating that he enjoyed the performance enormously, and that the exposure and publicity were very useful.

In the lead-up to this performance, the change from Mk I to Mk II had been handled with cloak-and-dagger secrecy akin to a Cold War spy novel, with Gillan and Glover joining the band before the outgoing Evans and Simper had even been told, with the farcical situation of gigs being performed by the Mk I band when it wasn't even the official line-up any more. Lord later admitted that he wished it had been handled better. Even on the night of the Concerto performance there was confusion, as the *Deep Purple* album had only just been released in the UK (to little fanfare as the band on the record was already defunct), and copies were given away as raffle prizes at the Albert Hall show. Gillan and Glover were bemused by requests for them to sign a new album which they weren't even on, despite having been playing live with the band for some months by that time.

Album Cover.
The cover design of the album deliberately echoed the style of many classical album covers of the period, with a photo of an empty Royal Albert Hall accompanied by the names of band, orchestra and composer at the top on a large white area. There was even a scholarly-looking note next to the name Deep Purple, reading 'In live concert at the Royal Albert Hall "Concerto For Group And Orchestra", composed by Jon Lord', above the large credit 'The Royal Philharmonic Orchestra. Conducted by Malcolm Arnold'. The inside gatefold of the album featured a monochrome spread of shots of the performance (musicians and audience), individual shots of the five band members and Malcolm Arnold in action and notes on each of the three movements by Jon Lord himself. Despite the somewhat dry nature of the front cover design (and the slightly jarring effect of having the names of band, orchestra and conductor writ large in purple, pink and red respectively!), the cover has proved to be somewhat iconic in its own way, and even prompted a homage of sorts from progressive metal band Opeth in 2010, when their live album *In Live Concert At The Royal Albert Hall* utilised an almost identical cover design, right down to the purple, pink, red large text at the top although on that particular occasion it read 'The Loyal Disharmonic Orchestra. Conducted By The Powers That Be'.

'First Movement. Moderato – Allegro.' (Lord)
The three movements of the concerto can hardly be considered 'songs' in the accepted sense, but nevertheless that is how we shall have to refer to them – and, at least vocals are a feature in one of them. Not so in this 15-minute instrumental portion, however, which sees the band and orchestra taking turns to play rather than too much in the way of full collaboration. It is described as Moderato – Allegro, which of course refers to the tempo of the piece; moderato means at a moderate pace while allegro means lively. An orchestral introduction takes up the first three or four minutes, before the band come in, assume dominance and then play unaccompanied for the next four minutes, before the orchestra come back in to reassert themselves. This sort of battle for supremacy was a key part of Lord's intention based on his notes about the piece, and it actually works extremely well for the most part. Some have criticised the orchestral sections for being overly simplistic or even banal, but this is an unfair criticism to level at someone composing way outside of his usual field of experience. To draw a literary parallel, Enid Blyton or Barbara Cartland may well have enjoyed the work of Agatha Christie, but one doubts

whether that would be enough for either of them to master the complex plot structure of a top-class detective thriller. In fact, the orchestral parts are quite adeptly done and even stirring in parts. The main criticism to be levelled at the movement is that for the most part it is more 'group or orchestra' than 'Group and Orchestra', as one tends to lie silent while the other plays. This is a shame, as the bridging sections between the separate parts, when they come in together on the main theme, are quite spectacular, and genuinely powerful. It is claimed that during the first group segment Blackmore extends his solo well beyond its prescribed length, taking the band into an improvised section leaving Lord to wonder whether he will ruin the whole thing. This is borne out by watching the film of the event, where a concerned-looking Lord casts anxious glances over at his errant guitarist, while conductor Malcolm Arnold appears to be waiting intently for his cue, and in fact leaps into animated life when it finally arrives! Ritchie was, as has been reiterated many times, unhappy with the concerto and, while he plays superbly in the service of it, one can easily imagine a typical streak of his rebellious mischievous nature prompting a small detour. A good start, though.

'Second Movement. Andante.' (Lord, Gillan)

Andante in this case refers to the tempo as roughly 'walking pace'. This second movement is notable as being the only one of the three to contain vocals, with lyrics written by Ian Gillan being the only non-Lord compositional contribution to the piece. Indeed, one wonders why Lord did not supply the words himself in order to have written the whole thing, as he had contributed words on previous albums. Nonetheless, the lyrics are thoughtful, intriguingly abstract, and crucially extremely sympathetic to the mood of the movement, which is far less brash and triumphal then the opening one. As Lord himself notes, the movement is roughly based around two separate melodies, which are played in various arrangements and permutations by the group and the orchestra. Gillan's vocal performance illustrates this, as he has two separate sections a few minutes apart, each one different musically as well as lyrically. In fact, his vocal is an excellent addition to this movement, sung in a lower register than much of his regular material and, if anything, bearing more of a resemblance to Rod Evans' style. The notes he hits are perfect however, with crystal clear pitch, and it demonstrates just what an exceptional voice he possessed at this time. The movement as a whole is more successful than the first, largely due to the fact that the group and orchestra play in unison for significantly more of the time, giving a sense of harmony rather than pitting them against each other in an effort to shoehorn them together. After the main vocal thrust of the movement is over, Lord's organ takes up the baton before the orchestra bring things home with a quiet section, almost fading away to nothing. This is in actual fact very often the sort of reflective role played by the second movement in a concerto or symphony, and illustrates that Lord was serious about composing a genuine concerto, rather than merely a 'piece' using the orchestra with the band. Twenty minutes of excellent music.

'Third movement. Vivace – Presto.' (Lord)

Vivace refers to an up-tempo mood to a piece, while presto refers to a tempo of 'very fast', so essentially these are the same thing expressed in a different way. Once again, as is commonplace within a piece such as a concerto or symphony, the final movement assumes a triumphant or dramatic feel, and this is surely deliberate on the part of Lord. After a powerful orchestral introduction, Blackmore and Lord take centre stage with a solo spot apiece, with Blackmore in particular excelling with some wonderfully expressive playing. The orchestra dart in and out of the group playing here in a playful and inventive way, and begin to work together as a disparate yet unified force better than at any other time in the work to this point. However, after six minutes, comes the one massive misjudgement of the whole performance; namely Ian Paice doing a drum solo. Now, Blackmore and Lord can get away with this as they are the only electric guitarist and organist respectively in the ensemble (plus, of course, Lord is the composer so can show off a bit), and also they are backed by the band and/or orchestra at the time. An unaccompanied drum solo just seems jarringly out of place, especially when the entire percussion section of the Royal Philharmonic sit idly behind him! Still, it is at least mercifully fairly brief, and orchestra and band return for a final, joyous 'free-for-all' together, as Lord's notes put it, before the final crescendo sends the audience into rapturous applause.

The Concerto has often been criticised and even ridiculed over the years, but this is grossly unfair. It is, if flawed, nevertheless a hugely enjoyable piece of music and a massive achievement for Lord, as a 'mere' rock musician. The film of the event shows the acclaim at the end, as a clearly enthused Malcolm Arnold calls Lord up to the conductor's podium to take the applause, before he himself urges the orchestra to their feet and brings the band up to him. Of course, it isn't the work that people remember Deep Purple for, and nor should it be in truth, but as an experimental divergence it bears favourable comparison with any big musical event you care to name from the time, be it the Who's staging of *Tommy* or Procol Harum's live album with the Edmonton Symphony orchestra. The Concerto itself was preceded by a short set by Purple alone, performing 'Hush', 'Wring That Neck' and 'Child In Time'; these recordings eventually surfaced in 1977 on the *Powerhouse* compilation, and we will deal with them later. One interesting aside is that there was actually an encore after the Concerto performance – and no, that didn't consist of another go through the whole thing! In fact, band and orchestra returned to play a five minute excerpt from the Third Movement again – including, yes that's right, the drum solo again! As baffling decisions go, that has to be up with the best – while almost any part of the work would be preferable to another drum solo, one would imagine that the vocal section of the Second Movement would be the logical choice, if only to showcase the full band again. But, it was what it was, and should not take the gloss off a tremendous evening. The next album, which was being recorded at this same time, would rewrite the rule book entirely, in a whole different way...

Related song.

'Hallelujah'. (Cook, Greenaway)

It is difficult to know where to put this one really, but as it was recorded by the Mk II line-up before the *Concerto*, it must go here. It was effectively the audition piece for Gillan and Glover, neither of whom had been officially inducted into the band until after the recording of this peculiarly out-of-character single. In fact, it is an excellent piece, characterised by some beautifully fluid and anthemic guitar playing from Blackmore and also Gillan's extraordinary performance: the band have said that they knew he was the one as soon as they recorded this, and it is easy to see why. Although by his own admission he was not overly impressed by the song on first hearing it, he makes it his own with a commanding performance, and the two 'screams' which seem to presage 'Child In Time' would surely have been the icing on the proverbial cake for the rest of the band. This was a very, very different proposition to Rod Evans, and they knew it immediately. The single was not successful (though it did make the Top 20 in Australia), and rather lazily had 'April Part 1' from the previous line-up slapped onto its B-Side, but it has turned up on the odd compilation of singles over the years. It deserves wider attention.

Deep Purple In Rock

Personnel:
Ian Gillan: vocals
Ritchie Blackmore: guitars
Jon Lord: keyboards
Roger Glover: bass guitar
Ian Paice: drums and percussion
Record Label: Harvest (UK), Warners (US)
Recorded October 1969 - April 1970, produced by Deep Purple.
Release date: June 1970. US release date: December 1969.
Highest chart places: UK: 4, USA: 143
Running time: 43:30

Album facts.

As alluded to in the previous chapter, the period leading up to the recording of this seminal work began with the most convoluted gestation period one could imagine, with two new members being virtually smuggled in under cover of darkness, as it were, while the band continued to honour gigs with the old pair without even telling them they were performing gigs with a line-up which didn't strictly exist anymore. Add to that the recording of the 'Hallelujah' single as an unofficial audition for Gillan and Glover, and then releasing it with a Mk I track on the reverse, and you could be forgiven for thinking you had stumbled into the plot of a far-fetched 1950s spy movie. Nonetheless, the skulduggery proved to be worth it in the end, as the Gillan / Glover pairing boosted the band's ranks immeasurably, and certainly put them on the road they had been itching to travel throughout the development of the earlier albums. Note that, from this album up until the Mk II split in 1973, all tracks would be collectively credited to all five members as co-writers.

The album itself was recorded at three different studios (IPC, De Lane Lea and Abbey Road) over a period of six months between October 1969 and April 1970, though in actual fact the recording work itself only occupied a couple of weeks or so of that time. The recording would be of necessity done on a piecemeal basis, with the band on a constant gigging schedule – both to recoup some money and also to tighten themselves and some new material up in readiness for the album – and also working on the *Concerto For Group And Orchestra* project. Such stop-start recording sessions could have adversely impacted the result but, in a way, it came to help the end result as the band were able to let loose all of their aggression and energy over these short bursts of creativity, and this give the album its astonishingly powerful and 'in your face' feel. The De lane Lea sessions were particularly notable as it was here that the band worked with engineer Martin Birch for the first time. Martin, who became to be known as 'The Wasp' by the band, almost became thought of as a 'sixth member', working on every album until the split in 1976. The band produced *In Rock* themselves, however. Chart-wise, the effect was double-edged as, while the album obliterated the band's desperately poor sales performances with the Mk I albums in their homeland by storming up to number 4 in the UK chart, America decided to react with a giant collective shrug, and the album limped to a paltry 143 in the US chart.

Album Cover.

One of the most instantly recognisable hard rock album covers of the '70s, the image of the band's faces overlaid onto Mount Rushmore in place of the presidents who actually occupy that monument was a stroke of design genius. In fact, this idea came directly from Purple manager Tony Edwards, who secured the band's agreement and then simply took the idea to London-based design company Nesbit, Phipps & Froome to ask if they could execute it. In keeping with the very basic design tools available at the time, the method used to accomplish this was simply to take photos of the band, cut out the heads, and stick them onto the background photo! The whole thing then had a quick paint job done to it in an attempt to blend the heads in with the mountain, which can easily be seen at a cursory glance. This somewhat rough execution aside, the image perfectly captured the mood desired, and is regarded as a triumph. The inside gatefold was monochrome, containing the album lyrics on the left panel, with brief notes alongside five individual photos on the right, and interestingly while the outside of the cover is laminated, the inner is not. One unusual and somewhat surprising feature of the packaging was that the front cover image was simply repeated, in exact duplication, for the back, which seems something of a waste. Even if ideas or time had run out, even something such as reversing the title lettering or just including the track and band listings would have been preferable, one would have thought.

'Speed King'. (Blackmore, Gillan, Glover, Lord, Paice)

As a statement of intent to open an album and herald a new line-up and new direction, they don't get much more direct than this one. Opening with a thunderous squall of chaotic noise from the whole band, a solo organ passage takes over as the thunder subsides, bringing some momentary peace before the band suddenly crash in with the opening chords of the song proper, including Gillan who enters at the exact same moment with the famous opening 'Good Golly said Little Miss Molly, when she was rocking in the house of blue light', heralding a lyric paying tribute to all of the great '50s rock and roll influences (the sleeve note describes it simply as 'a few roots – replanted'). From there it's an unstoppable roller coaster ride of a track, with the full-on aggression and energy only tempered slightly when Blackmore and Lord begin trading licks in a slightly more restrained instrumental section – but even this is short-lived as Blackmore's solo proper scorches in its intensity, leading the band into a dramatic ascending sequence building to a barely contained trademark Gillan scream before leading to a full-tilt assault on the first verse again, only with even more ferocity. Ultimately, the track collapses in a climactic crescendo sounding as if the band are simply too exhausted to go on playing. The line in the sand has been well and truly drawn.

However, it wasn't ever thus, as the first attempts at recording the song were quite different. The track had already been used as an opening number at the band's live shows for some months before the first attempts at getting it down on tape in October '69, and it was clear that the song was a natural opener for both album and stage show, but the earliest attempts at recording it had been in a much more subdued light, with one eye on a possible single release. Whereas the finished track used on the album is an organ-driven beast following the on-stage arrangement, the first recordings had Lord substituting piano for the Hammond organ, creating a much more subdued feel. Later turning up as a bonus track on a deluxe anniversary CD release of the album, this take isn't bad as it stands, but is rather disorienting after decades of hearing the original – it certainly highlights the massive contribution Lord's keyboards made to the Purple sound even when he wasn't taking a solo or doing any sort of 'grandstanding'. The intro is missing from this early version. Interestingly, for the first few months of the song's existence as a stage number, and even up until partway through the recording process, the lyrics were different and the song was known as 'Kneel And Pray', after one of the lines present at the time. The familiar chorus riff is instrumental in this incarnation, with 'Kneel and pray / Oh baby that is what I say' forming an extra bridging section back into the next verse. When the familiar version of the song was finally recorded, early in 1970, the opening section was recorded and saved to tape separately, and given the working title of 'Woffle'. This dramatic opening was omitted from the US pressings of the album, owing to a somewhat bizarre decision by the record company that listeners may be put off by the blitz of sound at the start! In actual fact, the inspiration for this opening came from live shows when the band had no chance to do a soundcheck – on these occasions, they would come on stage and immediately, in their own words 'make as much noise as possible' so that the sound man could at least have a go at getting his levels something like correct before the music proper began. From such ideas are legends born!

'Bloodsucker'. (Blackmore, Gillan, Glover, Lord, Paice)

This grindingly heavy mid-paced steamroller of a track was actually the last song written for the album, near the end of the recording process in April 1970. Clearly referring to a member of the opposite sex in less than flattering terms, Ian Paice has described Gillan's lyric as being one wherein he 'got out of his system' a lot of lines you might use with a girl. There was another contributory factor, however, which was to do with the band's management. Just before the song was completed, Ian Gillan had fallen out with manager John Coletta over a twenty pounds advance payment that he had asked for, and when asked for the lyrics he duly delivered them complete with bitter reference in the final verse to 'I can find a way to pay you back your twenty pounds'. It is not known whether Coletta was supposed to be the 'bloodsucker' of the title, though it is given the explanatory note of 'a particularly nasty sort of fellow – there are lots of us' in the album notes, so one can make one's own assumptions!

Musically, there is little unexpected about the track. It was reportedly written by Blackmore and Glover away from the studio, which was an unusual combination, and Glover's bass is certainly front and centre as he gives the track much of its oppressive heaviness. After the three verses, Blackmore comes in with a solo which is very much cut from his trademark cloth, before a short Lord solo brings back Gillan who shrieks the final verse (well, whichever verse it is, it is incomprehensible) in a tortured and almost demonically hysterical way, with Lord wringing some appropriately brutal sounds from the Hammond organ to match him. Definitely not a subtle track! The song was never played live – apart from a BBC session – but surprisingly was resurrected decades later for the 1998 Purple album *Abandon*, retitled as 'Bludsucker'.

'Child In Time'. (Blackmore, Gillan, Glover, Lord, Paice)

If any individual song can be said to encapsulate Deep Purple Mk II, this ten-minute epic would probably be it – along with perhaps 'Smoke On The Water' or 'Highway Star'. On an album whose chief mission statement is to show the band's identity as hard, heavy and powerful, 'Child In Time' is far and away the most complex and subtle piece in evidence. The structure of the song is well known to most people with a passing interest in the band – slow, reflective intro, building up to a crescendo along with Gillan's silver-throated screaming, before morphing into an iconic Blackmore solo, back into a repeat of the opening section, crescendo and big finish. What is also pretty well known is that there was an unashamed direct influence on the writing of the song – namely the track 'Bombay Calling' by American band It's A Beautiful Day. As has readily been admitted by the band, during an earlier US trip with Mk I Purple, the guys brought back with them some American albums which were not so easy to obtain in the UK at the time. One of these was the self-titled debut album by It's A Beautiful Day, who were led by electric violinist David LaFlamme. The album is probably chiefly remembered for the opening track 'White Bird', and 'Bombay Calling' was a less celebrated cut, but nonetheless Jon Lord began tinkering about with the song in rehearsals, and it gradually evolved into the beginning of what would become 'Child In Time'. This was some months before the recording of the album took place in earnest, as the song was – along with 'Speed King' – a staple of the band's live set from at least August 1969, and was certainly 'stage honed' by the time the band came to record it in November.

The third track to be recorded, it was always going to be difficult to replicate the song's onstage power and dynamism in the studio, but they undeniably did a fine job. Gillan's lyric is a triumph of economy, and leaves just enough open for the listener to interpret. By his own admission, it was written with the theme of the Cold War in mind, and he has said that when he heard that copies of the song had made their way into the hands of refugees in war-torn countries and brought them encouragement it was an extremely moving thing for him. In fact, the opening line of the song, and indeed the title, throw off the casual listener because of an implicit missing comma – there is no 'Child in time' in any mystical or metaphorical sense, it is in fact 'Sweet child, in time you'll see the line'. Of course, it could be argued that this in itself heightened the song's gravitas and appeal, so it may be that nothing is accidental. There are so many parts of this track which are genre-defining, from Gillan's scream vying with 'Won't Get Fooled Again' by the Who for 'greatest screaming in rock history, it has been said, through to the 'bolero' section bridging this rising crescendo to the instrumental part following, and of course Blackmore's guitar solo which has been hailed by many fans as one of his greatest ever. It was his greatest and most recognisable calling card to date, that much is undeniable. The very end of the song, with its speedy build up to a final long, fading chord, recalls the ending of the Beatles' 'A Day In The Life', a nod which Lord had admitted was intentional.

One interesting thing to note is that Blackmore's solo was recorded using his instrument of choice in the earlier Purple days, his Gibson-E335, in what was one of the last times he would use the instrument in the studio before switching his preference to his later trademark Fender Stratocasters. Oh, and as regards It's A Beautiful Day – the punchline to that particular story was that they opened their second album, *Marrying Maiden*, with an instrumental called 'Don And Dewey', paying tribute to the American rock and roll duo of the same name. The basis for the song? Why, that would be the main riff from 'Wring That Neck'! Roger Glover, in an interview with the author, has said that there might have been some tacit agreement between the bands, but whether that is the case or not, honour was seen to be restored without any unpleasant recourse to the courts. All ended amicably, without any need to 'wait for the ricochet'...

'Flight Of The Rat'. (Blackmore, Gillan, Glover, Lord, Paice).

A cautionary tale regarding substance abuse from Gillan here (the sleeve note proclaims 'Just to remind you there are other ways of turning on' after the song title, just in case we missed it). This was not an isolated case, as Gillan has stated on many occasions that the band all came from a 'drinking culture', and that hard drugs were never their game. Away from the lyrics, and the metaphorical rat's departure, the track is a fast, heavy, near eight-minute tour-de-force, driven by a relentless, and exhausting, performance from Paice. Indeed, the fact that the song was never performed live was attributed by Roger Glover to a reluctance on the part of the drummer, who he claimed always vetoed the idea on the grounds of the rhythm which he would have to keep up. This is entirely feasible, as the band have said that at this time their method for picking songs for the live set was that if any one member was strongly against playing a track live, they wouldn't do it.

The riff driving the verses is unusually propelled along by Glover's bass line, with Blackmore providing power chords over the top. There is just enough bounce and lightness of touch in this to prevent the track being buried under its own weight, which is a constant danger throughout this album, and one which the band just manage to negotiate. There are clever little tricks abounding, such as Blackmore's ascending flurry of notes to bridge one verse to the next, or the surprisingly funky little section near the end, prefaced by a short mini-solo from Paice, and which almost presages the direction of the Mk III line up (though more about that later). Blackmore and Lord both produce fairly intense solo passages, with Lord in particular sounding very much in the vein of his improvisations on stage, leading to the suspicion that both of the solos here may well be at least part improvised. An excellent start to the second side, taking the listener in an entirely different direction after 'Child In Time'.

'Into The Fire'. (Blackmore, Gillan, Glover, Lord, Paice)

'Out of the frying pan...' the sleeve notes inform us, not at all helpfully, about this, the shortest song on the album at around three and a half minutes. Lyrically this once again has 'Uncle Ian' delivering a stern warning to us about the dangers of those illegal substances. Indeed, on his own website, Gillan himself described this as 'a strange and innocent, yet incredibly powerful anti-drugs song'. While 'incredibly powerful' may be overstating this somewhat unremarkable lyric just a little, it does at least confirm his intention, and importantly his sincerity, when writing it. Musically there is a slight Hendrix influence again, but the more prevalent one is, unusually for Purple, that of King Crimson, whose debut album had been released just before this was written and recorded. In interviews with Stephen Clare, both Glover and Lord recall conversations with Blackmore about this great 'chromatic riff' he'd heard which, as Lord correctly suggests, is undoubtedly '21st Century Schizoid Man'. We're not talking about 'Bombay Calling' territory here, of course, but the riff undeniably has its roots in that particular Crimson piece, although Purple certainly take it in their own direction and develop it into something entirely different.

This was, surprisingly, the only track from the album apart from 'Speed King' and 'Child In Time' to make it into the band's stage set, where it remained for quite some time. Surprisingly for two reasons: firstly because it seems incredible now to think that the band were ignoring half of the album while keeping sprawling versions of 'Mandrake Root', 'Wring That Neck' and even 'Paint It Black' in the set. For sure, Purple at the time were all about improvisation and playing 'on the edge' every night, but three lengthy vehicles for those flights of musicianly abandon seems a little excessive with a hugely popular album sitting half ignored in the wings. Secondly, even allowing for that set imbalance, it seems odd that this track would be the one which would make the cut, as it is powerful enough but somewhat lacking compared to a couple of other sadly overlooked album tracks. Everything is perfectly good without having that – pun intended – spark to set it alight. The riff is grindingly aggressive, Gillan's lyrics are powerfully delivered and the guitar solo is well structured. But it isn't the most exciting track on offer by any means. Perhaps a clue might be offered by the fact that, soon after the album's release, Ian Paice noted that that the track seemed to be picking up a lot of airplay, perhaps because of its modest duration – it isn't beyond the realms of possibility that the band might have wanted to showcase a popular song. It's just as likely, however, that it might have been another case of a selection having to survive that dreaded 'vetoing' process.

'Living Wreck'. (Blackmore, Gillan, Glover, Lord, Paice)

'It takes all sorts – support your local groupie', announce the sleeve notes – giving a bit of a clue as to the genesis of this lyric. Clearly written about someone who has, to put it politely, 'seen better days', according to Ian Paice the idea came from one time when the tables were turned somewhat on Gillan as the object of his affections and amorous pursuit actually turned out to be a very experienced 'groupie'. The lyric seems unsure which way to go, as it simultaneously attacks the hapless subject in bawdy yet humorous fashion ('you took off your hair, you took out your teeth, I almost died of fright') while using the more melodic chorus to deliver some more considered words of concerned advice ('You'd better do something for your own sake. Yes it's a shame, ah you know you're a living wreck'). This approach actually works rather well, giving the impression of the singer using bravado to his colleagues while reserving some deeper concern for the lady in question, and keeps it from the realms of the gratuitous and superficial (which we shall come to shortly!)

Musically the track is a fairly brief and to the point four and a half minutes, based mostly on a heavy, mid-paced and fairly simple riff, though as we have said this changes and softens, along with Gillan's vocal melody, for the chorus. The track opens quite cleverly with a faded-in drum beat from the end of 'Into The Fire' which gives the impression of one leading directly into the other, when in fact they were recorded a month apart. A dramatic keyboard 'scream' (the only way to describe the tortured sound Lord drags from his instrument) leads us into the riff and we are away. After the first two verses Blackmore delivers a solo which is interesting if only for its method of execution. Sounding like a slide guitar solo, in fact he had been experimenting with an octave box, extending held notes as long as possible, and he plays all of the slide-sounding parts with his fingers alone. A third verse, a fairly generic solo from Lord and we are done. It's certainly another lesser piece in the grand scheme of the album, but to these ears more interesting than 'Into The Fire'. The song never made it into the setlist, but according to Lord was played at a couple of small pub/club gigs before it even had its title. All the more strange then that it was dropped thereafter...

'Hard Lovin' Man'. (Blackmore, Gillan, Glover, Lord, Paice)

Now, what were we saying about 'gratuitous and superficial' lyrical content again? Step forward the chief culprit on the album. Musically and lyrically, this is pure no-holds-barred, take-no-prisoners prototypical heavy metal. Beginning with another short 'cacophony' similar to the opening of 'Speed King', this dissolves into an insistent Glover bass figure before Blackmore comes in with a fast, galloping riff – the like of which Iron Maiden and others of that ilk practically built a career on, but here displayed as more or less the original blueprint. This isn't enough, however, as Lord piles on top with some of the filthiest, most violent Hammond playing ever committed to vinyl, hammering the song along like an out of control train. When Gillan comes in with the opening 'Break my back, with hard loving' then you know that, as Van Morrison once said, 'it's too late to stop now'! Following the first two verses it's solo time, and Lord duly obliges first, pulling out every trick from his onstage routine, wringing sounds from the Hammond that no-one else, outside of perhaps Keith Emerson, would even attempt. After this over the top display of virtuosic violence, Blackmore steps in, matching Lord step for step with his own display of barely controlled aggression, before it's back to the song proper again, with a clearly enthused Gillan bringing us back in with 'Come back here, it's not over', and it's plain that soulful, emotional feelings are not going to be on the menu tonight. After the final exhortations from the singer, who sounds as if he will need a rub down by the end, there is time for one last kick in the listener's beleaguered head as the music drops to leave Blackmore wringing hell from his tortured instrument in a display of pure 'Hendrix', before the band fade in again to complete the climactic effect before we are left with lingering squeals from Blackmore's rapidly surrendering Stratocaster. Then it's over, with the effect of the end of a particularly brutal show to match the beginning of the same at the start of 'Speed King'.

It probably played to the band's strengths that the album was recorded in such a piecemeal manner, as it is hard to imagine them being able to maintain anything close to this level of intensity if the had done everything in one short burst of daily activity. As it happens, when this track was recorded in January 1970, it was shortly before 'Speed King' was redone in its final form and the more sedate 'piano version' metaphorically ripped up. One does wonder whether the result of this closing assault led them to double down the aggression of their approach in terms of the opener. It does seem surprising that 'Hard Lovin' Man' was never attempted by the band on-stage at the time (despite a BBC session version being recorded), as it would appear to be exactly the sort of thing which would fit their dramatic, barely controlled stage persona like a glove. In fact, the track was finally given its debut some 39 years later, in 2009, to the surprise of all – especially considering the fact that the on-the-edge, violent aggression of these early days had very much faded and become tamed.

Related Songs.

'Black Night'. (Blackmore, Gillan, Glover, Lord, Paice)

Ah yes, the global monster hit single which almost never got written at all! The story behind this is that, once the album was completed, the record company asked 'what about a single then?', which was something the band had not considered. Having been dispatched to create something, they came back to the studio one evening from the pub, in a slightly inebriated state, and began jamming around a riff Ritchie started playing, which turned out to be from the Ricky Nelson version of 'Summertime', and a riff written by guitarist James Burton. This had already been borrowed once before, quite overtly, by American band The Blues Magoos, for their 1967 track 'We Ain't Got Nothin' Yet'. The band played around with the riff and started to refine it into something which sounded at once quite commercial but also of some merit. Gillan and Glover put their heads together and came up with, as Gillan later admitted, the most banal nonsensical lyrics they could think of. And with that, in around 30 minutes of creativity, under the influence of alcohol, a rock classic was written! After some eight takes (their playing was understandably somewhat sloppy), they left the studio reasonably happy but with no idea they had recorded something which would even be released, never mind a hit single. In actual fact this original version does sound a little leaden-footed and plodding in places now, but it is enlivened by some nice fills from Paice in particular, and is certainly catchy. Harvest records loved it, and it was released on the same day as the album, whereupon to everyone's surprise it climbed to Number Two on the UK singles charts (jostling with Black Sabbath's 'Paranoid' in the upper reaches at one point), and it earned the band their first *Top Of The Pops* appearances as the song hung around the charts for much of the year. It just shows, you never know what might be around the corner...

'Cry Free'. (Blackmore, Gillan, Glover, Lord, Paice)

A track which was recorded around the same time as 'Hard Lovin' Man' in January 1970, it was clearly seen as a real contender for the album as evidenced by studio records from the sessions indicating that there may have been up to 31 takes done of this one! Despite this, it still has something of an unfinished air, but that should not take away from the fact that this is an excellent track on its own merits, and perhaps only needed a little bit of production 'fairy dust' to lick it into album-worthy shape. This was not to be, however, as it was quietly dropped from the schedule towards the end of the recording sessions.

'Cry Free' eventually surfaced in 1977, on the *Powerhouse* compilation, and much later – with a Roger Glover remix to give it some gloss, on a 25th Anniversary CD edition of *In Rock*. It was well worthy of the public release, as it is propelled along dynamically on an insistent, driving riff from Blackmore, which was supposedly borrowed from an old Elvis record before being transformed through the mixer of the stage improvisations, as the guitarist would often throw it around during 'Mandrake Root'. Gillan sounds a little tentative, and doesn't really command the vocal, leaving the lyrics a little indistinct, though it is interesting to hear the tremulous high notes he hits in the chorus, almost warbling the title! A typically aggressive Blackmore solo adds to the entertainment value, though there is a slightly chaotic bit after this when the band appear to collapse in on themselves in a sonic heap before the next verse comes in and the song revitalises itself. Even if this wasn't going to make the album, it is difficult to see why it wasn't used as the B-Side to 'Black Night' instead of the somewhat unimaginative choice of 'Speed King' for the position. An extra well worth hearing!

'Jam Stew'. (Blackmore, Gillan, Glover, Lord, Paice)

As the title would suggest, this three minute instrumental which eventually saw the light of day on the 25th Anniversary CD was little more than a studio jam, based around a Blackmore riff which is fast and heavy, but a little more along the lines of a Bo Diddley sort of shuffle than the steamhammer *In Rock* riffery. It was recorded 'as live' in the studio, with the whole band playing together. As such, it wouldn't have fit onto the album very well but, again could have made a decent B-side. In fact, a version with some (probably improvised) Gillan lyrics was recorded for a BBC session about a month after this take was recorded, and in fact this BBC version is superior, being a minute or more longer and containing an extra, quite frenetic, Blackmore solo. It seems strange that the band would do that BBC recording if they had no intention of returning to the track, but such was the situation. Blackmore revisited the riff in 1971 when he played on the *Green Bullfrog* album, put together by former Purple producer Derek Lawrence, so he must have believed it had some promise, at least.

Fireball

Personnel:
Ian Gillan: vocals
Ritchie Blackmore: guitars
Jon Lord: keyboards
Roger Glover: bass guitar
Ian Paice: drums and percussion
Record Label: Harvest (UK), Warners (US)
Recorded September 1970 – June 1971, produced by Deep Purple.
Release date: July 1971.
Highest chart places: UK: 1, USA: 32
Running time: 40:30

Album facts.

Another album with a longer than anticipated gestation period, *Fireball* was originally planned for release before the end of 1970, but with recording going on from September 1970 right through to June 1971, it was July 1971 before the album finally appeared. Several studios were used during the recording period including De Lane Lea and Olympic Studios in London, but they also put together material at The Hermitage, Welcombe, North Devon, which was a big old house that Purple rented for seven weeks in order to prepare for the album. These sessions were apparently less than entirely productive, with Blackmore's well-documented practical joke penchant coming to the fore. Indeed, the normally mild-mannered Glover recalls chasing Blackmore and almost trying to kill him after the guitarist decided to smash his bedroom door down with an axe one night!

The first track recorded was the country-flavoured 'Anyone's Daughter', but another early completion was the hit single 'Strange Kind of Woman', which was included on the US version of the album but not the UK pressing. Most of the band have been critical of the album in later years, with Blackmore especially complaining that they were pushed into too much live work and not allowed enough time to properly prepare the album material. He also went on to comment at the time that he thought there were only three good tracks on the record ('No No No', 'Fools' and the title track), but this does seem an overly harsh assessment. The exception to this belief was Ian Gillan, who has gone on record many times over the years to claim that *Fireball* is his favourite Purple album, a view that he has attributed to the 'progressive nature of the music we were experimenting with', and also the freedom they had at the time to record whatever they wished to, within reason. The album was a huge success, reaching the Number One position in the UK (and also a much more respectable 32 in the US), but tellingly its stay on the UK album chart was significantly shorter than its predecessor.

Album cover.

The album cover, designed by Castle, Chappell And Partners, was another iconic image, with the front cover depicting the striking sight of the five band members' heads within a pink coloured fireball against a black, starry sky, hair flowing behind them, with the album title spelled out in the tail of the fireball itself. It's a great image, to be sure, but the rest of the package seems slightly lazy in comparison. Opening the gatefold out reveals the rear cover showing the earth with the tail of the fireball emerging from it, orbiting once and going around to the front, which is a good enough idea but a little dull. The inner gatefold is, however, a wasted opportunity, consisting of the exact same fireball image spread across the two sides, only this time in monochrome. There are a few credits and a smattering of monochrome band member shots, but it's a wasted opportunity, and somewhat close to the strange decision to make the rear cover of *In Rock* the same as the front. There was a lyric sheet with the early pressings, but it is not especially interesting to look at. This is a rare example of a gatefold cover which is more impressive to look at without opening it up.

'Fireball'. (Blackmore, Gillan, Glover, Lord, Paice)

A classic track to open proceedings, this driving, fast-paced rocker was to become a Purple standard over the years – though it would only remain in the regular stage set for a relatively short time after the album's release. The 'whooshing' sound, as of a fireball travelling by, which opens the track is actually an air conditioning unit being turned on, though the band tried to preserve the mystique a little when the album was released, informing the press when asked that it was a 'special synthesizer'! Following this, Ian Paice comes in with the drum showcase introduction, which is surely one of the most powerful and distinctive openings to a rock song ever recorded; it is an almost perfectly constructed and executed 'solo', containing a couple of stunning breakneck fills. The band come straight in after this, until after Gillan finishes with the lyrics another unusual ingredient is served up, with Glover contributing a short bass solo leading into Lord's brilliantly effective organ solo. Another repeated verse and chorus from Gillan and it's then fade out and end, all in just under three and a half brilliantly concise minutes. The lyric has been described by Gillan as a song about 'unrequited love' about a real-life girl who he described as 'a complete mystery to me', and despite that somewhat clichéd subject matter it does contain some of his most memorable lines, such as the timeless couplet 'Racing like a fireball, dancing like a ghost / you're Gemini and I don't know which one I like the most', and his claim that 'now I'm going with you down the road of golden dust', whatever that may be (it sounds impressive, anyway). The subject may be sex / love again (he did tend to gravitate to that old standby rather a lot), but it's much better in its execution than, say, 'Hard Lovin' Man'.

The track was released as a single, and reached number 15 in the UK charts.

Interestingly, the song features the first ever instance of Ian Paice playing a double bass drum and, some have said, virtually laying down the blueprint for speed/thrash metal in the process. He borrowed a second bass drum in the studio, which allegedly belonged to Keith Moon, who was recording with The Who in the studio next door. Whatever the truth of that, when they played the song live a roadie used to quickly add a second bass drum to Paice's kit, removing it after the song was finished – double pedals still being unavailable at this time – and it may well be that the inconvenience of this, added to the toll the song took on Paice physically, may have led to its being dropped from the set after the tour immediately following the album's release.

'No No No'. (Blackmore, Gillan, Glover, Lord, Paice)

This sprawling seven-minute track sees Gillan on a different lyrical track, as he gets into socio-political / environmental protest mode as he 'rages against the machine' to strong effect. Musically the track contains a strongly funky bedrock, from the introductory riff – repeated throughout – to the rhythm underpinning Blackmore's excellent, reverb-drenched slide solo. Indeed, listening to things like this illustrates that the funk influence which arrived with the Mk III line-up was nowhere near as left-field as some might have led us to believe. The verse riff is heavy, grooving and swamped in an utterly filthy, sleazy guitar sound perfect for the subject matter. Overall, it has to be said, it probably wears a little thin over its extended duration, and the chorus is rather over-familiar by the end – almost as if we have been hit over the head with the message – but like much of this album it is a brave, if slightly flawed, willingness to stray from the *In Rock* template which should be applauded. In the final analysis, almost fifty years on, in these days of environmental summits and the eco protest movement, lines such as 'Poison in the rain but they say, No no no we're not to blame' have never been more apt. This one was played in the regular setlist on the subsequent tour, but soon dropped thereafter.

'Demon's Eye'. (Blackmore, Gillan, Glover, Lord, Paice)

Jon Lord is the undoubted main man here, dominating this sprightly blues shuffle which strongly calls to mind the work of The Doors. Opening with a repetitive two-note organ figure, the band come in with the aforementioned shuffle rhythm, again owned by Lord, that drives the song along with much more swagger than the sluggishly paced 'No No No'. Blackmore gets a nod in by contributing an entertaining if safe (by his standards) solo, but this one coasts along on a bed of bass and organ for most of its duration. Gillan is on more familiar lyrical ground here, as he makes it plain to the woman pursuing him that he won't get burned again and that he cannot and will not trust her – the subtext here is that he has been hurt by her in the past and has his defences very much up. The Demon's Eye of the title has no fantasy or mythical overtones, she is simply described in the chorus as 'sly, sly / Like a demon's eye'. It's a nice track, but not one which contains any particular sort of depth,

45

and can come across as a little light and superficial depending on the listener's mood. The track was used as the B-side to the 'Fireball' single, but did not make it into the live set.

'Anyone's Daughter'. (Blackmore, Gillan, Glover, Lord, Paice)

Ah, the real divisive track whenever this album is discussed 'should it be on there, does it have any merit, is it just a novelty song,' etc. Well, at the risk of going against what may be the consensus, I'm going to say that I think it's a great song, and have always loved it (though I can understand why people would have the opposite view). Basically, it's a country-folk song with an amusingly told lyric from Gillan, but it is treated with a lightness of touch which is impressive from any rock band and has the wit and humour, not to mention the catchiness, to appeal to those who might normally dislike this kind of thing. Even Ian Gillan, the eternal champion of the album, says that this track was fun, but perhaps shouldn't have been on the album, while Blackmore has predictably derided it. Ironically, however, the song came from a Blackmore idea in the first place, as he was playing around with some ideas in the style of the great country/folk guitarist Albert Lee, of whom he was a great admirer. Indeed, Blackmore himself elevates the song above the ordinary with some beautiful pedal steel guitar licks, and it is he as much as Gillan who makes the track. Gillan has never been more disarming than on his delivery here of the tale of the hapless hero who gets in more and more trouble after dallying with the daughters of farmers, judges, but ultimately a rich man, and his casual asides ('it was nice..', 'hah - whaddya think of that?') bring the song to life. So – lovely change of pace or novelty waste of time – the answer is firmly in the ear of the listener. To these ears though, certainly the former.

'The Mule'. (Blackmore, Gillan, Glover, Lord, Paice)

A Deep Purple track like no other, this trippy, mantric almost-instrumental is the nearest they got to flat-out psychedelia. Ian Paice's repetitive, acid-tinged drum pattern repeats metronomically throughout the whole five and a half minutes, at first joined by Blackmore's similarly spacey-sounding yet evocative guitar riff. Gillan then enters with the sole verse, which again is a big change of direction from him, with its science-fiction inspiration. The lyrics are about the Isaac Asimov character The Mule, from his celebrated *Foundation* series of books – the greatest galactic conqueror ever seen, aided by the ability to subtly bend minds to his will. Gillan sings about being 'just another slave to The Mule', and has confirmed the Asimov-inspired subject matter on his website in response to a fan enquiry. After this verse Lord takes up proceedings with a keyboard solo taking things even further out musically, sounding reminiscent of an early Pink Floyd freak-out piece, by way of 'Tomorrow Never Knows' by The Beatles. Blackmore then takes up the cudgels, with a brief, bluesier interlude before Paice drives them toward the heart of the sun once again, with Blackmore going along for the ride. The last thirty seconds of this remarkable piece sees the track gradually imploding into a crescendo of chaos, before things die away. It may prove too repetitive for some, but for those who loved 'mind expanding' rock back in the day, it was to prove hugely popular. The track remained in the live set right up until the collapse of the Mk II line-up in 1973, but as a vehicle for a lengthy Paice drum solo, with only the initial riff and verse left to provide the connection with the original.

'Fools'. (Blackmore, Gillan, Glover, Lord, Paice)

Having had a little crack at spacey psychedelia on the previous track, this eight minute monster sees Purple indulging their prog rock side, right from the word go when Lord contributes a lengthy keyboard-led introductory sequence. Just as the listener is starting to get ever so slightly entranced by this stately instrumental passage, the band and Gillan slam in all together from absolutely nowhere on the first line with a brutal, anvil-heavy power-chord riff. Gillan's lyrics here absolutely match up to this dark, crushing mood as he clearly addresses the 'Fools' (the same ones as in 'No No No') who are leading this world into disaster, war, evil and environmental catastrophe. With imagery such as the Christ-like allusion to living and dying on a 'distant hill' to the 'blind and the child' crying (an echo of 'Child In Time') right through the climactic 'Please lead the way so the unborn can play on some greener hill / Laugh as the flames eat their burning remains, Fools die laughing still'. Yep, it's a long way from 'Anyone's Daughter' here, and we're not in Kansas anymore, Toto. Between the second and third verse there is an almost ambient section as Blackmore teases a solo out by delicately manipulating his volume control and fading each note up from silence, in an early execution of the technique. This only serves to ramp up the tension again as Gillan and his rampaging mob of funereal rockers crash in again for the final verse. As an exercise in light and shade it's a long way from most of what Purple were doing on *In Rock*, and in many ways a refreshing change. A little more of this kind of dramatic contrast could well have made that iconic album better still.

'No One Came'. (Blackmore, Gillan, Glover, Lord, Paice)

Another track which is all about the groove to close the album, as the band hit their stride straight away with an insistent, irresistible loping rhythm and simply never let up. Gillan's lyric is one of his very best ever; in his autobiography he states that it was inspired by his ever-present fear that one day no audience would show up, but it goes way beyond that to deliver an acerbic, satirical yet devastatingly accurate swipe at the pitfalls of fame and being in a rock band in the public eye. Essentially, it's like the later Pink Floyd line 'oh and by the way, which one's Pink', but analysed and dissected over three lengthy verses. There's humour aplenty here ('where's my Robin Hood outfit?'), but it all wraps up as the almost-climactic 'The money's good and the time you have, Fun and games galore / But you spend your money and lie in bed forgotten – And you wonder what you did it for' lays bare the real fear and insecurity behind the song. Vocally, the delivery is way ahead of its time, with Gillan's half-spoken, half-sung but perfectly rhythmic delivery anticipating rap music by decades – in a good way I may add. After the vocal half of the song is done, Lord takes things up with a brilliant keyboard solo which rides the groove so perfectly that you almost feel as if the track could go on forever, or at least until the very end when some ill-advised backwards piano comes in somewhat intrusively and hurts the mood at the fade out. Altogether though, possibly the finest track on a much underrated album. Certainly there are partial missteps in 'No No No' and 'Demon's Eye', but there is some great, adventurous material contained in this one and, while it isn't the finest Purple album, Gillan certainly has a point. Disappointingly for fans at the time, neither 'Fools' nor 'No One Came' were ever played live by the original Mk II band, though 'Fools' was resurrected some thirty years later.

Related Songs.

'Strange Kind Of Woman'. (Blackmore, Gillan, Glover, Lord, Paice)

Favoured over 'Demon's Eye' for the US version of the album, this track became one of the band's most successful singles when released in advance of the album in February 1971, reaching Number Eight in the UK charts, and immediately finding its way into the setlist for the band's live shows. The story related in the song is straightforward (boy meets girl, girl is hooker, boy doesn't care, girl falls in love with boy, girl gives up lifestyle, boy and girl get married, girl dies – you've heard it a hundred times; or perhaps not), but who the song is about is less clear. At live performances (captured on the album *Deep Purple In Concert*) he would often claim it was about a friend of his, but on other occasions he has described it as being about himself, and an almost adolescent crush he had on the woman in question. It has been speculated that the idea of her being a 'working girl' is instead an oblique reference to deeper issues in their relationship, but the fact that the working title of the song was supposedly 'Prostitute' would tend to support the obvious interpretation! Whatever the truth, the lyrics tell the story well in an engaging fashion, and the song bounces along well on a bluesy, uptempo sort of rhythm. Not a 'rock classic' per se, perhaps, but as an example of a rock song with the commercial potential to appeal across the board, it is a perfect example.

'I'm Alone'. (Blackmore, Gillan, Glover, Lord, Paice)

The B-Side to the 'Strange Kind Of Woman' single is something of a throwaway track, to be honest. If clatters along happily enough, driven by a Paice drum pattern reminiscent of 'Chasing Shadows', and in fact sounds more like a Mk I track than anything the band had done since 'Hallelujah'. The lyric is a concise pack of clichés which, within its three short verses, sees Gillan travelling on a lonely road which, naturally, leads nowhere. After rolling on for years with the sun his only friend and all his money, of course, spent, he finishes up by announcing, to nobody's surprise, that he 'feels like going home'. 'Fools' or 'Child In Time', it is not. Blackmore and Lord chip in with decent enough, if unspectacular, solos, and we're all done in three minutes. To be fair, as a B-Side it does the job, but it would never have fit on the album.

'Freedom'. (Blackmore, Gillan, Glover, Lord, Paice)

This out-take from the album sessions, which was appended on to the 25th anniversary CD issue, is basically Purple having fun vamping around on a '60s rock and roll vibe. Coasting in on a riff more than a little similar to Roy Orbison's 'Pretty Woman', every good-time rocking trick in the book is thrown into the mix here, from Gillan delivering a lyric which reads as if his dictionary contained only the words 'honey', 'money', 'trying' and 'crying', to Lord's tinkling barrelhouse piano solo, it essentially does what it says on the tin – fun enough, but no substance whatsoever.

'Slow Train'. (Blackmore, Gillan, Glover, Lord, Paice)

Another out-take, but this time one with much more energy, driven along by a breathlessly fast riff – which Blackmore must have liked as he recycled it a decade later on 'Firedance' from the Rainbow album *Bent Out Of Shape*. Gillan's lyric is somewhat difficult to comprehend, as he seems to be addressing a woman who he knows is bad news yet cannot keep away from, but he throws some largely unintelligible yet intriguing lines in the last two verses. Some great instrumental work from Lord and Blackmore midway through this one as well. Much better than 'Freedom', and if finished up properly there is certainly an argument that it could have fit onto the album proper.

Machine Head

Personnel:
Ian Gillan: vocals
Ritchie Blackmore: guitars
Jon Lord: keyboards
Roger Glover: bass guitar
Ian Paice: drums and percussion
Record Label: Purple Records (UK), Warners (US)
Recorded December 1971, produced by Deep Purple.
Release date: March 1972.
Highest chart places: UK: 1, USA: 7
Running time: 37:25

Album facts.

Honestly, can there be anyone with even a vague interest in the subject who doesn't know the story behind the recording of this album? Documenting it in the lyrics to the band's most famous song, 'Smoke On The Water', will tend to do that. The bare bones, and the common knowledge, is that they travelled to Montreux to record it, but the place burnt down during a Frank Zappa show and Purple ended up relocating to a hotel where they recorded the album with the Rolling Stones Mobile Unit. However, there is more meat to the story than that. The reason the Zappa show was so significant was that it was the last gig at the Montreux Casino before it closed for the winter break (4 December 1971), during which downtime Purple were scheduled to record there. The band travelled out in time to see the show, which was sold out, but more people were still trying to get in. In their infinite wisdom, the Casino security staff elected to padlock the side doors (essentially, chaining up the fire exits!), leaving the front doors as the only point of egress in an emergency, and thus creating a serious bottleneck. To compound this situation, someone had shown up in the audience carrying a flare gun, though how that was permitted in by these hapless security personnel is another question. To compound this still further, the ceiling was stuffed with incredibly flammable dried reeds. Straight away a picture starts to form, doesn't it?

So, this clown with the gun elects to fire it into the ceiling. Just as the synth solo in the song 'King Kong' started, though that is of no real significance. Apparently this was done with no malice, but instead just to cause some sort of 'happening'. There may have been no malice, but there clearly was an overdose of stupidity, but there it was – the whole place went up like a firework factory, leaving the crowd panicking as they tried to get out. Zappa quite courageously stayed onstage until the last possible moment, helping to direct people to the exit. The man in charge of the Casino complex was Claude Nobs, future Montreux Festival organiser for decades and immortalised as 'Funky Claude' in the song. The line 'he was pulling kids out the ground' may seem odd, as if these 'kids' were somehow embedded in the soil like so many giant golf tees, but no – there is a reason behind that line. There were apparently kitchens in a basement area under the stage, and a group of youngsters had headed down there in the hope that there would be another way out which, like any good stranger-than-fiction disaster story, there wasn't. They weren't even safe there since, as Ian Gillan puts it in his autobiography, 'smoke being heavier than air they were trapped down there'. Nobs managed to track them down and made a host of trips up and down the stairs to rescue them, eventually getting them all out safely. There were, amazingly, no fatalities, but that was partly because the stage had a large plate glass window next to it, and several of Zappa's roadies hurled speaker cabinets through it allowing people to use it as another exit.

The hotel that the band eventually decamped to (after an abortive attempt at a theatre called The Pavilion, from which they were evicted by angry locals complaining about the noise!) was the Grand Hotel, which was empty for the winter. The arrangement with the mobile studio was less than perfect as they apparently had to engage in a trek through kitchens, across landings, out onto a balcony, through reception and seemingly everything short of finding the source of the Nile simply to get to where they could hear a playback! Despite all of this – or maybe even because of it, in some decidedly British 'spirit of the blitz' bonding effect – they produced work of astonishing creativity. Plus they managed to get a sound which for the first time they were all happy with. By playing in a corridor. Yes, it's strange how things turn out sometimes, isn't it? Blackmore has even said that the spontaneity of the sound was helped by the fact that, such was the arduous journey which had to be made to listen to what they had just recorded, they ended up often just declaring a take the one to keep without hearing it back, because they simply couldn't face the journey!

The album was completed remarkably quickly, in the first half of December, and released on 25 March 1972, whereupon it became another Number One success in the UK – even reaching a lofty Number Seven in the US, who seemed to be catching up with the band again. The album was again self-produced by the band and, significantly, was the first of their albums to appear on their newly set up Purple Records label imprint. In the US it was still Warners. The now-familiar label design was a simple purple background with a large while letter P coming from the label edge and going around the centre hole.

Album Cover.

Like the previous couple of albums, *Machine Head* came in a laminated (external only) gatefold sleeve which was interesting yet once again a bit frustrating. Designed by Roger Glover along with manager John Coletta, the front cover showed the band reflected, in very distorted fashion, in a sheet of metal which was stamped with the band name and album title. It's an interesting image, but once again the reverse is a disappointment, showing the other side of the metal (the title is stamped in reverse), but this time the headstock of a guitar is reflected there, as if to hammer home the origin of the title (which, of course, refers to the tuning mechanism and peg on the guitar headstock). Inside there is a large collage of small square photographs spread across both sides. These are all manner of band and studio photos, as well as a multi-panel shot of the casino burning – but you guessed it, it's all monochrome again! Some blank panels for the track names and credits completed the design, except for a tri-fold lyric sheet / poster which came with the early pressings.

'Highway Star'. (Blackmore, Gillan, Glover, Lord, Paice)

No disrespect to 'Speed King', but with 'Highway Star' Deep Purple finally nailed their perfect show opener. Six minutes of pure greased lightning, an ode to speed and thrills, this is one of the great archetypal rock 'driving' songs. Think 'Radar Love' by Golden Earring, and 'Born To Be Wild' by Steppenwolf, then throw that disc out of the window because 'Highway Star' has entered the room and it wants to take your car keys!

The first 35 seconds of this track are some of the greatest seconds in rock history. Opening with Blackmore's power chords like sheet metal across Glover's thrumming bassline, the feeling of power and speed ramping up is enhanced by Paice's metronomically accurate drumming joining the fray, followed by Gillan's drawn-out 'Ahhhhhhh...' rising in volume. Then, just as the tension has built to an almost unbearable level as if the listener's head is about to explode, in come those two big chords and bang – the tension is released and the car is hurtling down the highway as Gillan comes in with the immortal 'Nobody gonna take my car...' opening. Truly stunning. If the track had just opened with the riff coming in it would still have been good, no doubt; but it is this opening half minute that raises it to true greatness. We're not done yet, however, as first Lord and then Blackmore in turn deliver two of the most recognisable and influential solos of the decade. There is simply no let-up, as even the odd breather of a few moments as the song transitions into or out of a solo seems merely like changing gear in order to accelerate again. It's six minutes, but it goes past like three. Basic it may be, but nobody ever said that rock had to contain a host of time changes and diminished jazz chords to achieve greatness – or if they did, they just have to hear this.

Amazingly, the song in its most basic form was written off the cuff on a tour bus. The band were on their way to a show at Portsmouth Guildhall in 1971 when a member of the press on board happened to ask Blackmore how he went about writing a song. He simply replied 'like this', picked up his guitar, and started playing the core structure and riff of what would become 'Highway Star'. Gillan, sitting next to him, began improvising lyrics along the lines of 'We're a rock and roll band / We're on the road again', and they knew they had something. The song was tidied up in the dressing room before the show and immediately included in the set that night – albeit in a rudimentary form with rather different lyrics. Blackmore has said that the chord progression behind the solos is taken heavily from Bach, though it is hard to hear the influence without very careful listening, as Johann Sebastian is fed through a cement mixer.

The lyrics are at the same time basic yet utterly iconic. In the space of three verses he eulogises about his car, his girl and his head (which is full of the thrills generated by the first two). Everything is compared to his car and, ultimately, speed. He is, in a real sense, the ultimate 'Speed King'. The whole lyric only includes about forty or fifty different words, so it is certainly no 'Stairway To Heaven' or 'Supper's Ready', but it doesn't need or try to be. It says what it has to then accelerates away from you. And there's no way you got the license number...

'Maybe I'm A Leo'. (Blackmore, Gillan, Glover, Lord, Paice)

Certainly a lesser track among such stellar company, 'Maybe I'm A Leo' is a fairly basic blues-based plodder which relies more on the feel and groove of the track than anything particularly outstanding. Paice is, as usual, in excellent form, as he keeps the aforementioned groove locked down solidly, and does what he can to propel things along, but things do begin to grow a little stale over the five minute duration of the song. Blackmore's solo is itself uncharacteristically muted. Glover, who wrote a lot of this track, has said that he was inspired by John Lennon's 'How Do You Sleep' when writing the main riff, and there is certainly a similarity of laid-back feeling to both of these creeping blues songs.

It is unclear as to who wrote the lyrics, but since Ian Gillan was the only band member with the star sign Leo, it must be a reasonable supposition that it was he. Once again, there are only three verses, but this time it is much more concise as each of these verses only contains three lines! From this brief nine-line tale we can deduce that he has returned after an indeterminate time to find the woman who used to be there has gone, much to his dismay. The second and third verses show us that he blames himself for his behaviour, and seemingly declares this out of character for him since, even though he is a Leo, he 'ain't a lion'. The slight confusion comes in the first verse when he exclaims 'they've taken her away', which seems at odds with the rest of the song indicating she has left him. Several theories exist, from it being his mother, and her having passed away since he left home after a fight, to suggestions that she was arrested after the violence that erupted between them. Ultimately, however, it simply isn't all that significant. It's a filler track – enjoyable filler, but filler all the same.

'Pictures Of Home'. (Blackmore, Gillan, Glover, Lord, Paice)

Definitely a 'deep cut' on the album, often undeservedly overlooked when discussing the record as it is in fact a terrific track. 'Pictures Of Home' finds Deep Purple at their most poignant. The lyrics, written by Ian Gillan while in a state of combined isolation and homesickness – exacerbated by the wintry December conditions – are full of imagery conjuring winter, loneliness and despair, with such evocative lines as 'I'm alone here / with emptiness, eagles and snow', and 'My body is shaking, anticipating, the call of the black footed crow'. There is also a generous helping of insecurity not dissimilar to 'No One Came' as well, as he declares 'Year after day I have grown / Into a hero, but there's no worship / Where have they hidden my throne?'

A fine lyric, certainly, but to bring out its full effectiveness it needed the right kind of musical backing, which was duly supplied by Blackmore creating a driving 6/8 shuffle rhythm with a marvellously icy guitar line riding over the top of it. The track is irresistibly propulsive yet still retains the fragile, wintry feel that the lyrics evoke so well. Ritchie has stated (notably on the *Classic Albums* TV show) that he came up with the guitar line while listening to a short wave broadcast from Eastern Europe – he believes it may well have been Bulgaria. Whatever it was, he took it and made it unmistakeably his own. Jon Lord also contributes valuably to the feel of the track with his great keyboard solo, including some rippling 'icy wind' effects. He also employs a recurrent technique of his, which is to hit one very high note on the keyboard, and hold it while he plays the solo or melody with the other hand – listen for it, it's one of his signature 'tricks'. The beginning of the song is introduced by another astonishing Paice drum intro similar to 'Fireball', which perfectly leads into the guitar riff, and towards the end of the song Glover even gets a short bass solo, which leads, via some more premium Paice fills, into a breakdown to a false ending, which bubbles back up as if emerging from some kind of whirlpool, taking the band into a final minute of instrumental coda.

Bizarrely enough, 'Pictures Of Home' was the only track from *Machine Head* never to feature in the live set at all at the time, with Blackmore for some reason known only to himself refusing to play it. Years later, after Steve Morse joined the band, it became a live staple, finally receiving its due place. Jon Lord has gone on record as saying that it was probably the best song on the album, and he may well be absolutely correct. While some of the more regularly played tracks might lose their sparkle over time, 'Pictures Of Home' has never lost that glitter of winter sun on alpine snow. Brilliant.

'Never Before'. (Blackmore, Gillan, Glover, Lord, Paice)

Another somewhat lesser track here, and yet one which was released as a single. In fairness, it is a catchy and fairly short track. It wasn't anywhere near remarkable enough to make it big in the singles charts, and only managed to limp to a disappointing Number 35 in the UK. Released on 18 March 1972, a week before the album, the song was initially put into the live set but, after its poor showing commercially, it was quickly dropped, along with 'Maybe I'm A Leo', leaving 'Highway Star' as the only song from Side One of the album to be in the live shows.

The track opens with a strange, somewhat aimless, funky jam (again giving the lie to the theory that funk was only introduced by Glenn Hughes), before morphing suddenly into the direct, rocking riff underpinning the verses. If anything it is too simple, since it seems to serve mainly to underscore the vocal hook melody that Gillan is singing. This then goes even more overtly commercial with the double-tracked chorus. It's quite good in itself, but it alienated much of the audience simply because it sounded as if it was aiming squarely for that chart success – perhaps unfairly in a way, since the same allegation could easily be levelled at 'Strange Kind Of Woman', which escaped any such opposition.

In a sense the most interesting part of the track is the short, reflective mid-section, the music for which was, according to Blackmore in the *Classic Albums* documentary, written by Jon Lord. Gillan comes up with a wistful vocal, reflecting on how this 'cold' woman had hurt him when he was younger. Double tracked on the vocal again, it sounds very much like a mid-period Beatles melody. This leads directly into a Blackmore solo, over another slightly funky backing, and then it's back to the verse and on to the end. It's a nice, commercial rock track, unchallenging, unobjectionable but, ultimately, unremarkable. And if there is one thing that the Purple audience would not forgive at this time, it was anything 'unremarkable'... though we can safely say that is not something often levelled at the Side Two opener, up next.

'Smoke On The Water'. (Blackmore, Gillan, Glover, Lord, Paice)

Ah yes, here we are. The riff learned and played (incorrectly, according to Blackmore) by a million beginner guitarists. Lyrically, of course, we need not tarry here, as the subject is a retelling of the story behind the making of the album. Musically, however, there is more to it than just that four-chord riff.

The song begins with another clever opening sequence, building in a similar way to the opening of 'Highway Star' before it. Blackmore gets proceedings underway, picking the riff unaccompanied (played in 'all-fourths' tuning, apparently, guitarists out there), before Paice enters with some subtle hi-hat accompaniment. Next up he introduces the snare drum to the beat before Glover joins in with a rumbling, monotonous bassline which must surely rank as one of the simplest yet most effective ever recorded. A trademark tasty roll from Paice brings in Gillan and the rest of the band in perfect fashion – another masterclass in how to open a song with the maximum tension and anticipation. The chorus is etched into the brain of any listener with the slightest interest in hard rock, of course, but as Glover says in the *Classic Albums* documentary, that in itself contains a bit of subtle genius. As he explains, when the opening two phrases of the chorus come in ('Smoke on the water / A fire in the sky'), your brain naturally expects the same two phrases again, as a regular four-part sequence. However, those subconscious expectations are subverted when the third phrase ('Smoke on the water...' again) instead leads directly to the riff coming straight in, the unsettling effect of which gives the riff much more power than it would have had if it had re-entered proceedings when the listener unconsciously expects it to. Very, very clever song construction indeed.

Blackmore's solo in the track is another of his most noteworthy, not because of any dextrous displays of speed and blinding technique as are many of his other best moments, but instead because it is beautifully constructed and phrased and, especially in the closing section of the solo, incredibly memorable. It lodges itself in the brain as securely as any catchy chorus, which is rare trick for any solo. The song was immediately massively popular, far beyond the expectations of the band, who saw it as something as a lesser cut when they first recorded it, and of course it has gone on to become a staple of every Purple performance since. It has also been a regular in the setlists of Gillan, The Ian Gillan Band, Rainbow (in the '80s) and even Black Sabbath, during the relatively brief time Ian Gillan was with them. It is one of those songs, like 'Stairway To Heaven', which has almost become bigger than the band. It was released as a single a year later in many countries (though not the UK), in edited form, as was 'Highway Star'. Both of these edits are a crime before God and we shall not speak of them again.

'Lazy'. (Blackmore, Gillan, Glover, Lord, Paice)

A strange sort of track this one. It is clearly written with the stage in mind, as it is largely an excuse for soloing and improvisation, but as a piece of music it doesn't hang together as well as much of the rest of the album. The track begins with an admittedly quite impressive, unaccompanied keyboard showcase from Lord, before Paice and Blackmore come in to deliver some aimless guitar noodling before deciding to finally give us the riff proper after just over two minutes. The main meat of the track then begins, and it is nothing more or less than a fast blues shuffle; the kind of thing one imagines the band would be able to improvise around in their sleep by this time. For the next two minutes we are treated to Blackmore delivering some nice licks while vamping around in a blues scale for a while. They are good licks, for sure, but there's really nothing new to see here. Lord gets in on the action as well, but not in any spectacular fashion. After four minutes of the total seven, Gillan enters with three verses berating an unknown third party for how 'lazy' he is. That's all. Nothing else. Oh, and in between these three verses (yes, three verses again!) we get some harmonica thrown in by Gillan himself, as if to hit us relentlessly over the head that this is a blues, lest we had become bereft of the power of genre identification. Vocal section done, it's then over to Blackmore to solo again for another minute or so, before they all dissolve into a clichéd bluesy (yes, you guessed it) ending. To be honest, it sounds like something along the lines of 'Jam Stew' which was originally played to warm up or let off steam but which they ultimately cleaned up for inclusion on *In Rock*. Whatever the truth of the matter, it became a live fixture, largely due to the fact that it became a traditional 'solo spot' number, which is its true home, if truth be told.

At just under seven and a half minutes, it is comfortably the longest song on the album. Whilst quite diverting for what it is, that does seem somewhat excessive – though of course it was extended beyond this in live shows.

'Space Truckin''. (Blackmore, Gillan, Glover, Lord, Paice)

For the closing track on the album we have a return to heavy, powerful rock. The 'building intro' trick is repeated again, this time with just bass and drums opening for the first 30 seconds, with Paice again bringing it to life. The song proper features fairly basic heavy verses, enlivened by Gillan's occasional falsetto screaming (not used here half as much as it was on *In Rock*, you will note). The key section here is the chorus, with Gillan's 'Come on, Come on, Come on' propelled along by a devastatingly propulsive Blackmore riff – which he has claimed was reminiscent of the theme to the 1960s TV show *Batman*. Following the brief lyrics, another funky instrumental break comes in (note again: there is much more funk than you remember in Mk II Purple!), before another classic build with slashing power chords, rising organ and finally one astonishing extended roll from Paice brings everything crashing into one massive release in the final chorus. Some 'outro' screaming of 'Yeah, yeah, yeah, space truckin'' by Gillan, take us into the end and fade, again on that riff. All done in four and a half powerful, compact minutes – though as we shall soon see, live versions soon turned into lengthy extravaganzas of twenty minutes and more, as the song replaced the old 'Mandrake Root' and 'Wring That Neck' improvisation vehicles. Sometimes for the better, but other times decidedly not; but such is the nature of the improvised beast.

The lyrics to 'Space Truckin'' are, of course, utter hogwash, but then again even Gillan has admitted they were never meant to be taken seriously. The Apollo Space Program was heavily in people's minds at the time, and any references to space, astronauts and planets all seemed very topical. There is a neat nod to the band themselves in the line 'The Fireball that we rode was moving / But now we've got a new Machine', though it has to be said that there is not, and never has been, any excuse for the line 'And every naut would dance and sway', with the later 'The freaks said / Man those cats can really swing' only a short way behind it. But then, that's Ian Gillan for you – he could be a great, intelligent and concise lyricist, but he could also come up with the most ludicrous piffle. It has always been the rough with the smooth with Gillan.

Related Song.

'When A Blind Man Cries'. (Blackmore, Gillan, Glover, Lord, Paice)

A delicate, achingly sad ballad, this short but quite exquisite song was recorded during the same album sessions, but once it was finished Blackmore decided, for reasons best known to himself, that he strongly disliked it – so much so that it was left off the final album tracklist. Ian Paice, in the *Classic Albums* documentary, says it was 'a crime' that it was left off, and Gillan agrees with him. Roger Glover, for his part, comments that it was an important song in that, as much as 'Smoke On The Water' tells the literal story of the recording, 'When A Blind Man Cries' captures much of the spirit of the often difficult time there, with relations between Gillan and Blackmore in particular beginning to break down.

Gillan himself has said that the title came to him to symbolise the fact that, no matter how low you may get, there is always someone worse off than you and, as he says in that same documentary, 'When a blind man cries you know something's really wrong'. The lyric is in fact achingly poignant, telling of the loneliness of said blind man when he is left alone and hopeless after his 'friend', who brought him a 'good time' has gone and left him alone. Blackmore's guitar solo is absolutely sublime, and almost tear-inducingly mournful, which makes it all the stranger that he disowned the song. In fact, it was only played live once at the time, and that was at a single gig when Blackmore was ill and Randy California from Spirit deputised.

As if that wasn't evidence enough of the regard for the song from the other band members, it has been proven beyond all doubt by the fact that, since Ritchie left for the final time in 1993, it has assumed a renewed life of its own. Put into the setlist as soon as Steve Morse joined on guitar, in 1994, it has remained there ever since, being regularly extended to twice its original three and a half minute duration, and featuring a full band coda of great effectiveness. Since the advent of the CD, reissues of *Machine Head* have routinely included the track, and it is now viewed as the 'unofficial eighth track' on the album.

At the time, however, it was pretty much buried, appearing only on the B-side of the unsuccessful 'Never Before' single. It was introduced to a wider audience in 1977 as part of the *New Live And Rare* EP, along with the live version of 'Black Night' from the *Made In Japan* shows and the unreleased track 'Painted Horse' (see chapter *Who Do We Think We Are*)

Made In Japan.

Personnel:
Ian Gillan: vocals
Ritchie Blackmore: guitars
Jon Lord: keyboards
Roger Glover: bass guitar
Ian Paice: drums and percussion
Record Label: Purple Records (UK), Warners (US)
Recorded 15-17 August 1972, Osaka and Tokyo, produced by Deep Purple.
Release date: December 1972 (UK), April 1973 (US).
Highest chart places: UK: 16, USA: 6
Running time: 76:44

Album Facts.

It may seem hard to believe today, but *Made In Japan*, one of the definitive and most highly regarded live albums of all time was almost released as a Japanese-only 'afterthought'. The band's popularity over there was at a high after *Machine Head*, and the band were approached by Japanese record company representatives to record a live album for their market. Strange as it may seem, given the band's reputation as a live act, they had never really given any thought to a live album before this. They agreed to the recording, on the basis that it was going to be only for the Japanese market, but insisted that if it were done it should be done properly, and specified that the three shows, at Osaka on 15/16 August and Tokyo the night after, should all be recorded and the best material from all three shows selected for inclusion. When they finally heard the playback of the recordings they were impressed at the quality of them (even though only Glover and Paice took part in the mixing), and it was quickly decided that the album should receive a world-wide release – and the rest, as they say, is history. Gillan, for his part, was critical of his own performance, but agreed that the overall quality was excellent, while Lord has gone as far as to declare it his favourite Deep Purple album.

The album, on double vinyl, included the whole of the band's regular set, but did not include any of the three encore songs played. We shall come to these shortly.

Album Cover.

The cover of the album was designed by Roger Glover, and featured colour photographs of the band on the front and back, surrounded in a striking gold background, while the inner gatefold was made up of a red and orange 'rising sun' design, with monochrome photos and credits included. The track listing and other credits were in the sun itself, with the photos in between the 'rays'. There is a slight 'cheat' with the photos, as they were actually taken in London, and not at the Japanese shows at all, as might be assumed. The back cover photo was taken at a show at the Brixton Sundown – now the Brixton Academy

– and in attendance at this show was a young Phil Collen, later to be with Def Leppard. Look closely and he can actually be seen in the audience in this back cover photo, watching Blackmore.

The Japanese release was identical, but came in a different sleeve design and was titled *Live In Japan* (we must assume that the 'made in Japan' joke, referring to the mass production of consumer goods there for export to the UK, would have been lost on the Japanese audience!). The front cover had a different photo, taken from above and behind the band, and is quite impressive. As well as a lyric insert (Japanese live albums often had these, though they were sometimes, shall we say, less than accurate) and handwritten messages from the band, the first pressings contained the very unusual extra of a 35mm film negative containing photos of the band which fans could print themselves if they wished. Other releases were more or less the same worldwide, with the bizarre exception of Uruguay, who released it as a single album, with only sides one and two, in a unique cover with a rising sun design on the front.

'Highway Star'. (Blackmore, Gillan, Glover, Lord, Paice)

Recorded at Osaka, 16 August. Regarded by many as the definitive version of this track, it begins with some ambient tuning noises from the band before they begin a similar 'build-up' introduction as on the *Machine Head* original. The make-up of this intro is quite different, and less subtle, as is to be expected from a live performance, and is in some ways closer to the *Speed King* 'wall of sound' opening. There are similarities, however, with Blackmore's power-chording still in attendance, and Paice's insistent drum pattern moving things up another gear (if you will pardon the pun) when it comes in. Lord and Blackmore's solo spots are similar to the original, but ramped up greatly in intensity. It is clear that there have been no overdubs or retrospective 'fixing' going on, as is the case with many live recordings, because there are a couple of missed notes in Blackmore's solo. Far from detracting from the effect, however, it rather enhances it, with the realisation that this was exactly how it was played on the night itself making the playing all the more impressive.

'Child In Time'. (Blackmore, Gillan, Glover, Lord, Paice)

Also recorded at the Osaka 16 August show, which was felt to be the better of the two shows at that venue. No introduction necessary here, as the audience applaud furiously at the first keyboard notes. Gillan is on exemplary form, eclipsing even his performance on the original. The combination of his astonishingly clear yet dramatic 'screaming' with the redoubled intensity of the band make for one of the heaviest and most crushingly powerful performances ever witnessed. Blackmore's solo is possibly even better than his much-praised studio original, and when the band stop on the proverbial dime at the end of this section the effect is stunning, with the audience clearly astounded. There is a really nice addition during the second sung passage, after Blackmore adds some subtle 'volume swells' on the guitar, with the line 'wait for the ricochet' answered by a recording of billiard balls cannoning into each other – one of those additions for a live recording which is henceforth oddly missed when listening to the studio original. It is only marred by Gillan's unnecessary declaration of 'I wanna be inside you' at the same time! After the steamrollering of the big 'scream' section again, we are treated to another, shorter, guitar solo, together with some almost unintelligible improvisory interjections from Gillan, beginning with 'You're only about four foot six, but don't worry about it. There's always somebody smaller than you'. It has been suggested that this could be some reference to Ronnie James Dio, as his band Elf first supported Purple around this time, but there is no evidence to support this.

Thus endeth arguably the greatest recorded version of 'Child In Time', in all its twelve and a half minute glory. It is hard to imagine it being improved upon.

'Smoke On The Water'. (Blackmore, Gillan, Glover, Lord, Paice)

Recorded at the 15 August Osaka show – the only track on the album to be taken from this performance. The 15 August show was generally accepted to be the weakest of the three shows overall, while the Tokyo show, although by all accounts a superb display, was not as well recorded. This performance, however, is far superior to the one at the second Osaka show, and hence it was selected (also Blackmore's intro, where he tended to have fun twisting the riff, diverted just a little too much for the record company's liking on the 16 August performance). The song is introduced by Gillan explaining that it told the story of the *Machine Head* album, 'and what went wrong when we did it', before the band replicate the building intro from the studio version extremely well – in fact, the moment when Glover's bass comes in delivers even more bottom-end power than the original. Blackmore's solo is excellent, though he does hit one suspect chord during the riff just before it. You can never tell with Ritchie's playing, but it does sound a little like a mistake – though once again, that only enhances the superb playing during the solo.

At the end of the final chorus, the song is extended by around another minute or so. Gillan ad-libs a little, Jon Lord contributes a brief solo, and the whole thing climaxes with a short 'call-and-response' section between the guitar and keyboards before the band crash in with one of the best power-endings ever executed. It's a tremendous version.

'The Mule'. (Blackmore, Gillan, Glover, Lord, Paice)

One of only two tracks used from the Tokyo show on 17 August. As previously noted, the recording was not entirely of quite as good technical quality, but this and 'Lazy' were deemed fit for use. Fans of the studio rendition of this track might be disappointed, however, as we only get a minute and a half of the main riff, with Gillan delivering the lyrics in cursory throwaway fashion, before Ian Paice treats us to a drum solo lasting for over six minutes. Great player that he is, it's hard going. The band come back in with the riff at the end, and then it's all over. It's good, but not what it could have been.

Incidentally, this track is preceded by one of the most celebrated (and copied!) stage asides of all time, as Gillan is asking for a bit more volume in the monitors, and Blackmore can faintly be heard suggesting they have 'everything louder than everything else', which Gillan takes up and repeats gleefully. This famous phrase has since been appropriated by Meat Loaf and Motorhead, to name two, for song and album titles respectively.

'Strange Kind Of Woman'. (Blackmore, Gillan, Glover, Lord, Paice)

Back to Osaka on 16 August now, for this rendition of the non-album cut 'Strange Kind Of Woman', slung out in much heavier and more confident, swaggering style than the original. Gillan is clearly enjoying himself, having fun as he puts everything he has into the lyrics, even dissolving into laughter during the final chorus. Two storming solos from Blackmore, and we're in 'definitive' territory again, up until around five minutes in. Then things go off the rails a little, with some of the celebrated Purple 'improv', which could be brilliant or ... less so. The latter is the case here, as Gillan's weak asides ('she was so bad...' 'evil', 'she was the worst thing you've ever seen' etc) lead us into an extended 'call and response' section between guitar and vocals which, while cleverly done, tries the patience at over three minutes. The band come in again briefly, only for Gillan to display a screaming demonstration which, again, is impressive but does not make for great listening. At nine and a half minutes, it's four and a half too long.

'Lazy'. (Blackmore, Gillan, Glover, Lord, Paice)

Tokyo again, for around eleven minutes of exactly what you expect you're going to get. Yes, it's a whole festival of flexing the instrumental muscles, and hard to deny that it's a little overdone. Lord opens proceedings with three minutes of keyboard showcasing, with a little assistance from Paice toward the end. Then Blackmore joins the party for another minute of somewhat aimless noodling, before the band come in with what we might call the 'track proper' from about four minutes. The vocals don't begin until a mammoth six minutes in, and then we get that darned harmonica again (you can imagine the after show conversation: 'I saw Deep Purple tonight' 'Wow, great – how was the harmonica?'; or maybe not). A minute and a half later and Lord and Blackmore are embarking on another two-man self-satisfaction party, until the band get going again for the last minute or so. When they play they are very tight. But if ever you wanted to play something to a younger fan to illustrate the more bloated aspects of 1970s live shows, you might think about playing this. Or something by Led Zeppelin; it's a tough call.

'Space Truckin''. (Blackmore, Gillan, Glover, Lord, Paice)

Osaka 16 August again, for what would appear to be even outdoing 'Lazy' at its own indulgent game, with a *twenty* minute version of 'Space Truckin'', quadrupling the original studio length. This, however, is more successful, being the sort of full-band improvisation perfected over the years of 'Mandrake Root' and 'Wring That Neck', and there is genuinely thrilling stuff here after the song itself crashes to an end after five excellent minutes. Lord and Blackmore are totally on the edge here, threatening at any moment to go over but always retaining their balance, so to speak. It's like listening to the equivalent of a man crossing Niagara Falls on a tightrope, and almost but not quite falling. It's not perfect, of course – this sort of thing rarely is, as demonstrated over the years by acts as great as Cream, the Allman Brothers and, yes, Zeppelin – but it's pretty darn good all the same. Blackmore even throws in a snippet of 'Jupiter' from Holst's *Planets* suite, decades before the same part was adapted for the Rugby Union anthem 'World In Union'. A couple of minutes around the quarter hour part drag things somewhat, but this is recovered entirely as the band skate around utter disaster for the final few astonishing minutes, before things just die away, leaving the audience silent for a few seconds as they clearly try to process what they have seen and heard. A perfect climax to the album.

Related Songs.

'Black Night'. (Blackmore, Gillan, Glover, Lord, Paice)

Three songs were played as part of an encore each night, but none were included on the original album. With the advent of CD, a double-disc version was eventually released containing the encores on the second disc. Long before this, however, this superlative rendition of 'Black Night' appeared, firstly as a single B-side in some countries (not the UK), and then included (as a very successful piece of 'fan bait') on the budget priced compilation *24 Carat Purple* in 1975. It later appeared as the 'live' section of the *New Live And Rare* EP.

After a minute or so of ambient Lord-led musings (not included on the earlier edit but left intact on the CD), the music suddenly begins ramping up, with Gillan's 'it's a thing called 'Black Night!'' sending the audience into raptures and signalling the band to hammer into the familiar riff as if they were starving dogs suddenly having been thrown a pound of sausages. The rather sterile feel of the original is eclipsed here, with Paice in particular filling every available space with driving drum fills, giving it a momentum the original never had. The instrumentation is clearly all very loud, overdriven and barely under control as well, imparting an energy to the whole thing which is utterly infectious and irresistible. Blackmore and Lord both contribute storming solos, and the whole thing never lets up for five adrenaline-fuelled minutes. This track practically had its own fan club with mid-'70s schoolboys who'd heard it on *24 Carat Purple*, and no wonder. Not only is it easily the best recorded version of 'Black

Night', but one of the standout performances in the band's career. It is still hard to fathom why it was absent from the original album, when one considers that a six-minute drum solo was included and the whole thing was still less than 77 minutes long!

'Speed King'. (Blackmore, Gillan, Glover, Lord, Paice)

Some encore! Straight from that assault on 'Black Night' into 'Speed King' – not exactly giving themselves a respite, for sure. This and 'Black Night' were both recorded at the Tokyo gig, and selected for good reason as they are probably the best of the three nights' versions. 'Speed King' initially sounds a little stilted after the adrenaline rush of 'Black Night', but once the solos start coming the intensity is raised massively, and by the end the roof is being audibly raised. There is a part a couple of minutes in when Gillan starts telling some 'mothers' to 'sit down and let the people enjoy themselves', which we can only assume to be some over-zealous security personnel, as it is hard to imagine Deep Purple midway through an encore of 'Speed King' in 1972 imploring the crowd to sit down! The song is introduced in the beginning as 'a bunch of old rock and roll numbers stuck together', and Gillan comments that it was 'originally done to raise some perspiration, but now we're doing it to stop ourselves drowning', so it must have been fairly warm up there.

'Lucille'. (Little Richard / Albert Collins)

Back to Osaka for the third encore, and the only disappointment among them. They seem to be having fun but, along with other bands who used to feature rock and roll medleys or songs at the time, such as Uriah Heep or Led Zeppelin, it always seems a lazy and sloppy way to finish rather than playing something else from their own impressive catalogues. For Purple's part, an eight minute version of this old Little Richard number, no matter how enthusiastically played, seems somewhat like eight wasted minutes when the band have tracks like 'Fireball', 'Hard Lovin' Man' or 'Pictures Of Home' in their locker. Still, it is perhaps a little picky to complain about a third encore, and the crowd do seem to enjoy it.

Overall, despite some slight missteps on the likes of 'The Mule', 'Strange Kind Of Woman' and 'Lazy', *Made In Japan* remains the best example of Purple's live power to this day, and is rightly regarded as a benchmark among live rock albums.

Shades Of Deep Purple – original 1968 UK cover. *(EMI)*

The Book Of Taliesyn, 1968. You'd never guess it was the '60s... *(EMI)*

Deep Purple (third album), 1969. Note band lurking below harp. *(EMI)*

Concerto For Group And Orchestra album cover, 1969. *(EMI)*

Original programme from the Royal Albert Hall *Concerto* performance, 1969. *(Dougie Currie)*

Royal Albert Hall

24

Sept., 1969

To be Retained   P.T.O.

6/-

Arena
(Standing)

Ticket stub from the original *Concerto* performance at the Royal Albert Hall, 1969.
(Dougie Currie)

The iconic, if poorly executed, *Deep Purple In Rock* album cover, 1970. *(EMI)*

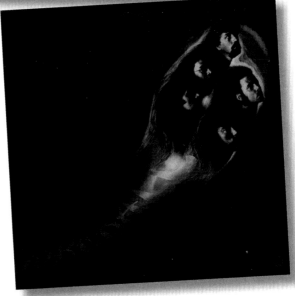

Fireball album cover, 1971. *(EMI)*

Machine Head
album cover, 1972.
The big break...
(EMI)

The 'gold standard'
for 1970s live albums.
Made In Japan original cover,
1972. *(EMI)*

Original Purple Records *Who
Do We Think We Are*, 1973.
The wheels begin to come
loose. *(EMI)*

Ritchie Blackmore and Ian Gillan in a rare jovial moment, 1973.

Ritchie Blackmore in close-up on stage, 1973.

Above: Ian Paice signed
drumsticks and skin.
(Dougie Currie)

Right: Deep Purple ticket
1974 - note support band!
(Dougie Currie)

Harvey Goldsmith for John Smith
Entertainments in association with
Purple Records presents

Deep Purple

IN CONCERT WITH

E L F

T H E   A P O L L O
Renfield Street, Glasgow

MONDAY, 22nd APRIL, 1974
at 7.30 p.m.

STALLS

G   N⁰   29

Ticket £2.00 inc. V.A.T.
TO BE RETAINED

The original Glenn Hughes bust used for the *Burn* candle mould. *(Par Holmgren)*

Stormbringer album cover. It finally got its deserved gatefold with the 35th Anniversary vinyl reissue. *(EMI)*

Made In Europe original UK gatefold sleeve, with enthusiastic use of font... *(EMI)*

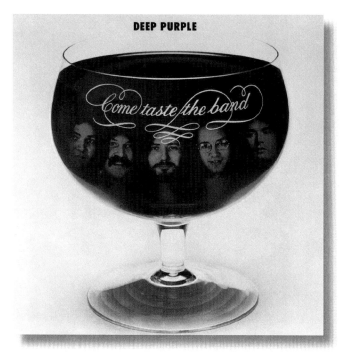

Come Taste The Band
album cover, 1975.
(EMI)

Deep Purple 1976 USA tour programme, bought at the final Liverpool show where excess copies were sold. The signature is David Coverdale. *(Author's Collection)*

Deep Purple 1976 UK tour programme. *(Steve Richardson)*

Deep Purple badge from Wembley 1976. *(Steve Richardson)*

Inner spread from the 1976 USA tour programme. *(Author's Collection)*

A very well-thumbed copy of the purple vinyl *New Live And Rare* EP, 1977. *(Author's Collection)*

Above: David Coverdale on stage with Purple Mk IV in Japan 1975.
Below: Tommy Bolin in action with David Coverdale, Japan 1975.

Demo copy of the first Rainbow single, 1975. *(Dougie Currie)*

Rainbow ticket from the 1976 *Rising* tour. *(Dougie Currie)*

The vibrant cover of the *Ritchie Blackmore's Rainbow* album, 1975.

Rainbow UK tour programme from the 1977 *Long Live Rock 'n' Roll* tour.
(Author's Collection)

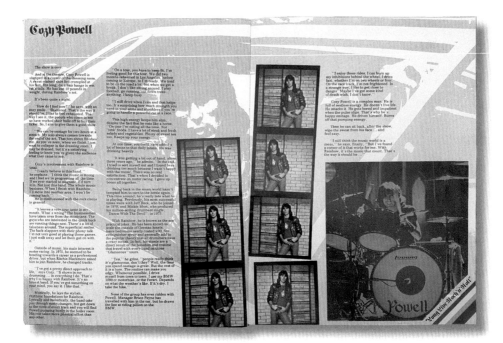

Inner spread from the Rainbow 1977 UK tour programme. *(Author's Collection)*

Rainbow On Stage original UK cover, 1977. *(Polydor)*

The suitably epic *Rainbow Rising* front cover painting, 1976. *(Polydor)*

Rainbow badge from the 1976 *Rising* tour. *(Steve Richardson)*

The rather underwhelming *Long Live Rock 'n' Roll* cover, 1978. *(Polydor)*

Rainbow see out the 1970s with Graham Bonnet on *Down To Earth*, 1979. *(Polydor)*

Rainbow 1977
backstage passes, with
bassist Bob Daisley's
signature.
(Dougie Currie)

Who Do We Think We Are.
Personnel:
Ian Gillan: vocals
Ritchie Blackmore: guitars
Jon Lord: keyboards
Roger Glover: bass guitar
Ian Paice: drums and percussion
Record Label: Purple Records (UK), Warners (US)
Recorded July and October 1972, produced by Deep Purple.
Release date: January 1973.
Highest chart places: UK: 4, USA: 15
Running time: 34:27

Album Facts.
Who Do We Think We Are was, by common knowledge, an album with a difficult history, with relations within the band, particularly between Gillan and Blackmore, becoming ever more strained. Indeed, around this time Blackmore himself had been making some noises about possibly leaving the band, as he had been playing with Ian Paice and Thin Lizzy's Phil Lynott in an unnamed trio, and he was keen to address this and other projects. In the end it came down to a 'him or me' situation between him and Gillan, a situation which was forcibly resolved when a burnt-out and weary Gillan announced his own resignation at the end of 1972. He was persuaded to stay on for a further six months to fulfil touring plans after the album's release, and Deep Purple Mk II played their final show (at least of the '70s) in Osaka again, somewhat fittingly, on 29 June 1973. Roger Glover, who had also somehow got caught up in the crossfire, left at the same time. About Glover's firing, Ritchie Blackmore has said that he felt bad about it, as Roger had done nothing wrong, and had reiterated his own desire to leave instead of causing a double firing, but with Gillan going it was clear that the band didn't want their prize asset to go anywhere, and acquiesced to his desire for a new 'clean slate' of vocalist and bass player, to join the core three, and take things in a slightly bluesier direction – another story which will be addressed soon.

In an interview with the author, Roger Glover claimed that the last words Blackmore spoke to him for several years were as he passed him on the stairs before that last Japanese show: 'I'll never forget it. He passed me and simply said "It's not personal, Roger. It's just business", and that was that.' On the subject of his firing, he revealed that Jon Lord did actually talk to him and Ian Paice about the possibility of carrying on with a new singer and guitarist, at the time when Blackmore and Gillan were both threatening to leave. He said that it became apparent that there was more covert business going on during early 1973, ironically similar to when he and Gillan themselves joined: 'As the tour progressed however, I felt myself getting more and more frozen out of things, and not included in band discussions, so I confronted the management to see what was going on, and after initially denying it, they eventually admitted that Ritchie had agreed to stay in the band if I left, but they weren't going to tell me until the end of the tour to prevent me leaving beforehand – so it's obvious what a blow that was. I was told to finish the tour then leave the band, so that's what I did.'

Despite all of this bad feeling, the band did manage to put together a credible, if somewhat short, album, which is better than its reputation often leads one to think. Recording sessions began in Rome in July, before the Japanese tour where *Made In Japan* was recorded, but this less than productive spell only yielded two tracks – 'Woman From Tokyo' and the unused at the time 'Painted Horse'. The album was completed in October in Walldorf, near Frankfurt, again using the Rolling Stones Mobile Recording Studio, though unlike the Montreux experience this time the 'fireworks' were confined to the band members' relationships in the studio. There was substantial difficulty in agreeing on tracks for the album, and some parts reportedly ended up being recorded separately in order to keep people apart. Glover again slightly disagrees with this common view, however, and suggested, again to the author, that it was more like Paul McCartney's claim that *Let It Be* was 90% enjoyable, but people wanted to focus on the other 10%. He admitted that there had been some difficult times, but stressed that 'that's how it was with Ritchie - a lot of the time it was fine, we had a great time, and it was a really good dynamic, it wasn't these constant arguments that people imagine. The thing with Ritchie though is that while he's a great, gifted musician, he's not a natural team player.'

Album Cover.

Once again the cover of the album is designed by Roger Glover, with manager John Coletta (photography is by the noted rock'n'roll snapper Fin Costello). A quite eye catching image, the front cover has a series of bubbles floating up against a stormy sky, with the five band members pictured, in live performance poses, in each one. The title is in a matching bubble-shaped round design. It's gatefold, laminated and quite appealing. Of course, following the grand Purple tradition of no imagination, the rear cover depicts - yes - more bubbles. But without heads in them. The inner gatefold is much better, consisting of an array of press clippings about the band, some positive and some resoundingly negative. It shows the band's sense of humour, and there's lots to read there. The credits and track listing are there (with the tracks also on the back cover), together with a quote from Ian Paice in Melody Maker from 1972 which gives the album its title: discussing the heaps of letters, positive and otherwise, that the band receive, he says 'the angry ones generally start "Who do Deep Purple think they are?"'. There was also a lyric sheet insert with the vinyl, having the words in white on purple.

'Woman From Tokyo'. (Blackmore, Gillan, Glover, Lord, Paice)
The most well-known track on the album by some considerable distance,

'Woman From Tokyo' was released, in edited form, as a single in a number of countries including the US, but surprisingly not the UK, where no singles were taken from the album. The single release was scheduled for the UK, and even given a catalogue number, but for some reason this was shelved. Opening with Paice, once again, he is soon joined by Blackmore who plays the riff a couple of times, almost as a teaser, before meandering around for a short while. This is all to set up the moment when the band slam in together with the main riff, and does so superbly. The song is on the front foot immediately, and gains an instant momentum which it sustains for most of its almost-six minute duration. After a couple of verses and choruses we come to a quiet, reflective mid-section, with Gillan lamenting that he feels he doesn't belong now that he is home again, and some rather lovely piano from Lord takes things down almost to a dead stop, before a brilliant moment when the band storm in again with redoubled intensity. It's a rock classic for sure, only losing its way a little for the final minute or so when some strangely incongruous bar-room piano from Lord leads into some rather listless repetitions of 'My woman from Tokyo' and the whole thing kind of fizzles out. It might have been better to end it around a minute earlier – but then again, the album is only just over 35 minutes as it is, so they might not have had that luxury.

The words are often reported to have been inspired by the band's first visit to Japan, but this is not directly the case as it was recorded in July, a month before that inaugural Japanese trip. It may have been inspired by the anticipation of the Japanese shows, of course. Bizarrely, but in a way unsurprisingly given their track record in the area, the band never played the song live on the subsequent tour, and it did not receive its first live airing until Mk II reformed a decade later. One does wonder how this could possibly have been overlooked as a live number with its popularity as a single and also its immediacy, but then again there were those powers of veto by band members against tracks to play live, so we can only surmise.

'Mary Long'. (Blackmore, Gillan, Glover, Lord, Paice)

Almost as surprising as the omission from the live show of 'Woman From Tokyo' was the fact that this somewhat unassuming track WAS played live on the tour – not that it is a bad track, but there seems little to mark it out as a great 'live' song. The lyric was written by Gillan about the somewhat prudish and censorial attitude of older British people, exemplified by the bastions of 'public decency' at the time, Mary Whitehouse and Lord Longford. These names were amalgamated into the single composite character 'Mary Long'. An interesting subject, though in all honesty the words are sometimes clumsy and somewhat awkward, as in the 'How did you lose your virginity? / When will you lose your stupidity' chorus couplet. Nevertheless, there are some elements which bear explaining so long after the events. The accusations of 'hypocrisy' and reference to 'your friend the porny Lord' are chiefly directed at Longford, who was somewhat disgraced after being discovered attending strip clubs

67

while denouncing adult entertainment loudly in any form. The reference to the writing by 'Johnny', the 'waste of public money' and the line 'but everyone thought the show was funny' comes directly from the TV scriptwriter Johnny Speight, the creator and writer of the TV show *Till Death Us Do Part*. Remade in the US as *All In The Family* (where the main character's name was Archie Bunker), the show featured the central character Alf Garnett, the outspoken, bigoted anti-hero parodying the prevalence of such attitudes in working-class Britain in the late 1960s. Whitehouse was driven to near apoplexy by the constant 'swearing' of Garnett, even though the use of the word 'bloody' would hardly raise such ire by today's standards!

There is a tendency for the lyrics to overshadow the music in this case, partly as the subject matter is so unusual and direct, but also because the music is in itself somewhat unmemorable. It canters along on a nice enough riff, and the chorus is quite catchy, but it is certainly no 'Woman From Tokyo' when it comes to great moments lodging themselves in the brain of the listener. Again, there seems to be some padding at the end, as it begins to drift along rather anonymously towards its conclusion. It certainly isn't a bad song by any means, but as a single live showcase for the album it does seem odd.

'Super Trouper'. (Blackmore, Gillan, Glover, Lord, Paice)

A pretty dense heavy riff-driven track, which comes in at under three minutes – very short for Mk II Purple. The verses bear a distinct resemblance to 'Bloodsucker' from the *In Rock* album, but this bludgeoning effect is broken up by the more dreamy sounding chorus. Unfortunately, the rather heavy-handed phase/flanging effect of the vocals in the chorus tends to detract from it rather than enhance it, as it is laid on so thickly as to be distracting. It's a decent enough song, but not recorded or developed as well as it could have been, and it sounds more than anything else on the record like a casualty of the difficult working conditions which had crept in.

Gillan's lyric is interesting again, here. Beginning with the unexpected opening line 'I was a young man when I died', it appears to be inspired by characters such as Jimi Hendrix, dying young as casualties of the Rock And Roll lifestyle. The 'super trouper' of the title is this first-person character who talks about coming back and being 'like I was before' but this time resolving to 'know the score'. The track has some interesting lyrics and some good musical accompaniment but, in the end, is just a little less than she sum of its parts could have made it.

'Smooth Dancer'. (Blackmore, Gillan, Glover, Lord, Paice)

With this track, the lyrical gloves are entirely off as Gillan takes aim at Ritchie Blackmore with both barrels of this surgically incisive lyrical assault. As bitter and full of invective and spite as anything that passed between Lennon and McCartney at their most hostile, it is barely even veiled to anything more than a cursory glance. The 'Smooth Dancer' of the title is referred to throughout as 'Black Suede', a reference to the guitarist's famous choice of attire in his 'man in black' persona. Indeed, the very first line opens things up by declaring 'Black Suede, don't mean you're good for me', and he goes on to issue such stinging attacks as 'You've swollen up inside, With nothing but your pride' and 'Baby, you can rock 'n' roll, But you can never show your soul, smooth dancer', and in the ultimate defiant response to Blackmore's attempts to force him out or break him, announcing his decision to walk away, 'You'd better do it right because one day or night, I'm gonna walk to freedom / You know I loved you once and I want to love again, But you don't give nothing'. It's heavy stuff, and hard to believe that Blackmore did not realise or care about the message being aimed at him. It has been reported that the vocals were recorded without Blackmore being present, and that scenario is certainly eminently plausible.

With this lyrical spat going on, the music could – and in many reviews indeed has tended to – be overlooked, but in actual fact it's a fast, upbeat rollicking rock 'n' roll number displaying none of the darkness or menace suggested by the lyrics. Particularly in the verses, which are slung out effortlessly quickly by Gillan, there is a catchy, good-time rock sensibility that foreshadows some of the work of his own future band simply named 'Gillan' in the 1980s.

'Rat Bat Blue'. (Blackmore, Gillan, Glover, Lord, Paice)
Side Two opens with the five and a half minute 'Rat Bat Blue', with a Gillan lyric which takes the form of a somewhat sordid and distasteful account of the habit of using and discarding groupies. It is one feature of his lyrics from this period that, while he could be very thoughtful or genuinely amusing by turns, he also had a tendency to occasionally stray into slightly unnecessary and somewhat misogynistic territory. Not too often, fortunately – there wasn't a 'Hard Lovin' Man' on every album – but there's certainly one here. The first of the now customary three Gillan verses has him picking up said conquest at a show, the second has him perpetrating the dastardly deed, while the final verse has him essentially kicking her out of the door now she is no further use to him. Why, it even namechecks that infamous earlier song in the charming couplet 'Get out! You didn't understand / I'm a hard loving man, No way you can satisfy', before adding for good measure the parting shot of 'And when you shut the door, Make sure I don't see you 'round here no more'. Why Mr Gillan, you are quite the romantic soul, I do declare!

Musically the song is driven along on a catchy yet unremarkable Blackmore riff (he really is on auto-pilot for most of this album, it has to be said), and the chief point of note is the excellent extended Jon Lord solo, which presumably he got the space to do because there was no inclination for a guitar solo. No matter, as he fills the void beautifully, going through his whole repertoire of tricks. Starting slowly, the band pick up their heels with a dramatic shift in tempo, and the keyboards go chasing along joyfully in their wake. There is one slightly superfluous section in which Lord displays his undeniable abilities in a dazzlingly fast display which strays a little too close to novelty 'Flight

Of The Bumble Bee' territory for comfort, but he soon makes amends as he begins pulling out all of the Keith Emerson touches as he mangles all manner of tortured sounds from his groaning Hammond. It makes the song, without doubt.

Oh, and the strange title, while being something of an unsolved mystery, may have an explanation as it has been claimed to be taken from the name Ian Paice gave to a drum fill exercise that he used to warm up in the studio. So now you – possibly – know!

'Place In Line'. (Blackmore, Gillan, Glover, Lord, Paice)

Here's where the audience divides itself, and exclaims either 'great, a pure blues number' or, alternatively 'oh no, they've done a pure blues number'. Very much a case of your tolerance or capacity for straight-up, slow blues, but let's have a look at how they've filled in the six and a half minutes anyway (quiet at the back, blues-haters!).

Actually, the blues-haters would probably have a point here, because this really does reek of 'filler', especially at the length it is. It is essentially a run of the mill slow blues, sung by a po-faced deep voiced Gillan in a tone which is faintly ridiculous. They pick up the pace a bit now and then after the vocals are finished for the first time, and for Blackmore's solo, but it just becomes a mid-paced blues shuffle, which doesn't improve things much. Blackmore plays a decent enough laid-back blues solo, but then again he could probably play a decent enough blues solo in his sleep – which coincidentally is how this track sounds. It isn't a lost masterpiece, it simply isn't very good. It filled up a third of Side Two for them, though.

Gillan's lyric about standing in an endless line appears to comment on the futility of the rat-race, but the line about him having been standing in the line for 'nine long years' could indicate a reference to the music business, since at the time of recording that would take him back to his time starting out in the Moonshiners and the Javelins in 1963. It's not really worth dwelling on, though.

Oh, and yes. It has three verses...

'Our Lady'. (Blackmore, Gillan, Glover, Lord, Paice)

At last, closing a largely disappointing side of vinyl, comes one of the great 'lost' Deep Purple songs, and an outstanding 'deep cut' on the album. Along with 'Woman From Tokyo' this is arguably the strongest track on the record. Opening with Jon Lord's rising feedback, the song bursts into life with a beautiful chord progression pushed along by Lord's tremendously fat, deep organ sound. No razor sharp guitar riffs slashing across this one, just a big, full sound with a vocal melody and general feeling that nudges close to 'I Am The Walrus' in places. The backing vocals in the elegiac chorus are magnificent, and listening to the song on headphones can really transport the listener into the music. It is unclear whether Gillan's dense lyric is spiritually inspired or referring to something different, but it doesn't really matter. It's one of those songs where you get your own meaning out of it, and somehow that's all that really matters.

Doesn't have a guitar solo this one. Doesn't need one. Doesn't sound like typical Deep Purple. Doesn't have to. It's simply great music however you slice and dice it. Three verses from Gillan, to nobody's surprise, but hey – the last song on the last album by Mk II Purple, he wasn't going to change now, was he? It's a great closer to an era.

Related Song.

'Painted Horse'. (Blackmore, Gillan, Glover, Lord, Paice)

The only song along with 'Woman From Tokyo' recorded at the initial July '72 session in Rome, there are conflicting reports about the decision to leave this one in the vaults. It has been widely claimed that it was rejected because of Blackmore disliking it once again – which would be unsurprising – but there are also claims that the sticking point was Gillan's vocal on the track. Allegedly only Jon Lord of the other members was happy with the vocal performance but Gillan refused to redo it. Whichever story is the correct one, it is still a shame as this is a strong track. True, there is some harmonica which could be done without, and Gillan does sound a little out of character, but is has the groove and feel of an early Cream track, and by the end has drawn the listener in. Gillan's lyrics (*four* verses – maybe that jinxed it??) are intriguingly vague, with each verse seeming to be about death in a different form (a child, a carpenter, the narrator himself), but with the feeling that a deeper meaning lay beyond. We never find out why the titular Painted Horse is weeping, but like 'Our Lady', perhaps we don't need to.

At over five minutes it doesn't outstay its welcome at all, and would have pushed the length of the album up to 40 minutes. Instead it had to wait until 1977 to appear on the *Powerhouse* odds-and-sods compilation and also the *New Live And Rare* single along with 'Black Night' and 'When A Blind Man Cries'. Mind you, it is an odd fact that every Mk II studio album (and indeed even the double *Made In Japan*) had exactly seven tracks on it, so why change it now? An era was over, and it was time for a radical reinvention to occur.

Burn.

Personnel:
David Coverdale: vocals
Ritchie Blackmore: guitars
Jon Lord: keyboards
Glenn Hughes: bass guitar, vocals
Ian Paice: drums and percussion
Record Label: Purple Records (UK), Warners (US)
Recorded November 1973, produced by Deep Purple.
Release date: February 1974.
Highest chart places: UK: 3, USA: 9
Running time: 41:37

Album Facts.

With Gillan and Glover out of the picture, the stage was set for Deep Purple's most crucial line-up change yet. Good though some of the Mk I material was, and certainly improving by the third album, it is safe to say that the departure of these two made a much greater hole than Evans and Simper. Blackmore in particular was keen to follow a slightly bluesier direction, and as such he wanted a different type of singer to the vocal gymnastics of the very much non-blues Gillan. His first target was Paul Rodgers, who had recently departed from Free, but although he considered the offer he declined in favour of the band he was putting together, Bad Company.

Instead the first to join was West Midlands native Glenn Hughes, from Trapeze. The lead vocalist as well as bassist in that band, he was keen to fulfil the same dual role within Purple, but was also excited by the idea of Rodgers. When that route was closed off, the band still pursued their search for a dedicated lead vocalist, with the idea being to have Hughes share the vocals, and thereby give the sound another level of depth it had not previously had. They advertised the position, and watched the audition tapes roll in.

The man eventually selected was an unknown from the North East of England, David Coverdale, at the time working in a clothes shop, although with a previous band called The Government he had supported Purple at a show soon after the arrival of Gillan and Glover, ironically enough. There was much interest in this new man plucked from obscurity, as the press spun it, and they certainly milked it as a 'Cinderella story' – which, to be fair, Coverdale himself admitted was very much the case.

In a move which might have been seen as flirting with disaster, the band headed off to none other than Monteux, Switzerland in November 1973, with the Rolling Stones Mobile unit in tow. Luckily, however, no casinos were harmed during the making of this album and recording was completed within the month. Writing credits had now been reverted to actual participating composers as opposed to the 'all for one' system that the Mk II period had employed. This was at the insistence of Blackmore, who realised as time went along how much he was actually forfeiting in this way as he played such a large part of the writing process. All of the members contributed some writing, although Glenn Hughes was omitted from the credits on the initial release owing to contractual issues. On subsequent CD reissues he has been given the credits he is due.

The album was released in 1974 to a strongly positive reception from critics and public alike, and has gone on to be regarded as one of the band's strongest efforts.

Album Cover.

The album cover design was an instantly recognisable and very strong image, with the band represented by five individually moulded candles, lit and moodily shot with purple-tinted 'fog' drifting around the bases. The design was by the company Nesbitt, Phipps and Froome and the superbly crafted candles were specially made and supplied by the imaginatively named Candle Makers Supplies. The candles themselves are all 'headshots', with Blackmore being particularly recognisable in his trademark 'witchfinder' hat. The logo for the title, with the letters in the form of flames, was also notable. The rear cover showed the remains of the candles after they had burned down, with the band members' photos rising from them like disembodied spirits. A very clever design, only marred slightly by the lack of either a gatefold or printed inner sleeve.

It seems incredible that the obvious marketing opportunity of making the candles available for purchase was missed, but so it was. They were supposedly finally made available to buy for a short time around 2005 (42 years later!), but I have never seen one.

'Burn'. (Blackmore, Coverdale, Hughes, Lord, Paice)

An instant classic from the new line-up, and the song which was to be the live set opener for the next two years until the band dissolved in 1976. Opening with Blackmore's scything riff, accompanied by just Paice, another dazzling roll by the drummer brings the band in together in blistering fashion. Coverdale and Hughes trade vocals, with the former taking the lion's share – though in an interview with the author Hughes stressed there was no competition for vocal space at this time, saying that it was almost a case of 'You take this part; no, after you'. Blackmore sounds completely rejuvenated here after his audible disinterest with *Who Do We Think We Are*, and the solo he contributes here is probably his most impressive since 'Highway Star'. Not to be outdone, Lord chimes in shortly afterward with a dazzling keyboard solo of his own. Over the song's six minute duration, there is barely a second wasted. A rock classic in anyone's book.

The fantasy storyline lyrics were penned by Coverdale at Blackmore's request. Reportedly he drafted several alternative sets of lyrics, with the guitarist selecting the best. While clichéd for sure, the lyric fits the music like a glove. Interestingly, according to Jerry Bloom's Blackmore biography, the riff was inspired by a 1936 song by the Gershwin Brothers called 'Fascinating Rhythm', and a cursory investigation of this earlier piece does reveal a similarity. Not Bombay Calling this time, of course, but enough to support the alleged connection.

'Might Just Take Your Life'. (Blackmore, Coverdale, Hughes, Lord, Paice)

Notably, this mid-paced rocker was released as a single in the UK – the first domestic single release since 'Never Before' in 1972, though it did not chart (the US went for an edited version of the title track as a single, but the UK did not follow suit). The B-side was an unused track from the album sessions named 'Coronarias Redig', of which more later.

Opening with a plodding yet groove-laden riff which is slightly reminiscent of a bluesier 'Woman From Tokyo', Coverdale's vocal here gives the track a real sleazy, blues edge which simply wouldn't have been there with Gillan. This is a good example of what Blackmore wanted to bring in to the band's sound, although it must be said that Lord is the dominant instrumental figure here. Hughes takes a verse, but the track is far more suited to Coverdale's voice. The pair combine splendidly for the chorus, and Lord contributes a nice solo. The lyric is the first example of what would become something of a Coverdale trademark, of the 'drifter without a home and needing no friends' song. There would be many variations on the theme over the years.

'Lay Down Stay Down'. (Blackmore, Coverdale, Hughes, Lord, Paice)

If there is a 'lesser' track on the first side of *Burn*, this one would be it. Opening with a fast and heavy guitar riff, Paice's drumming immediately shines as he virtually performs a drum solo behind the verses. Not since the halcyon days of peak Keith Moon had a drummer attempted such outrageously wild and seemingly undisciplined playing and yet got away with it perfectly. The chorus, when it arrives, is a much less heavy, more boogie-driven affair, with the vocal melody searching for a more commercial quality that isn't quite there. After a strong opening, the song loses its way a little, needing a strong Blackmore solo to keep the interest up for the full four and a half minutes. It made it into the set for the subsequent tour, where it went over quite well as a 'fun' live rave up, as it were. The lyrics are not exactly Proust either, being a sort of paean to the groupie service which sits alongside Gillan at his most one-dimensional.

'Sail Away'. (Blackmore, Coverdale)

A complete change of direction here, as the first song on the album to really delve whole-heartedly into the soulful, bluesy feel and pretty much eschew the expected hard rock entirely. Credited to Blackmore and Coverdale only, the track has a tremendously sinuous and evocative groove to it, with Coverdale's lyrics conjuring up the need to 'sail away' from the bad times and bad things in your life and retain hope and belief that you will arrive at calmer and safer waters. Soulful swamp-blues at its best.

Coverdale excels here in particular, and it is easy to see where Paul Rodgers would have fit in had he elected to take the job. Hughes sings alternate verses, but his higher, more strident vocals don't sit on the groove in the same way as Coverdale's do. This is, of course, right in his comfort zone as not only is his voice ideally suited to this story of groovy funk-blues but the lyric is right in his personal wheelhouse as well, full of imagery of him 'drifting' and having 'no place to go', while accepting that he is 'gettin' old'. It's a fine song with which to close the side of vinyl, with some great bluesy soloing from Blackmore.

'You Fool No One'. (Blackmore, Coverdale, Hughes, Lord, Paice)

Driven along by an insistent, clattering Paice percussive rhythm slightly reminiscent of Led Zeppelin's 'Immigrant Song', this is a naggingly catchy track sung largely as an ensemble piece by Coverdale and Hughes in harmony. In fact, the track was initially inspired by Paice's drum pattern, and the guitar and bass give it a very funky edge – the only outright funk influence on the album really. It has a nice enough Blackmore solo, but it isn't really anything exceptional and soon becomes somewhat repetitive, with a rather by-the-numbers lyric concerning a 'my lyin' cheatin' woman done me wrong' kind of affair. Despite its unremarkable studio incarnation, the track became a live fixture until Blackmore's departure, expanding to become a vehicle for instrumental showcasing and often lasting for 15 minutes or more.

'What's Going On Here'. (Blackmore, Coverdale, Hughes, Lord, Paice)

The slightest song on the album in terms of its songwriting, this track is described by Hughes on the *Critical Review* DVD as something they put together in the studio as a somewhat throwaway bit of fun. Nevertheless for all that, it is an enjoyable listen. Indeed perhaps it is that very sense of fun which gives this simple song about drinking and high times its appeal. Blackmore sounds as if he is really enjoying himself, and his licks raise the track above the 'filler' level. Lord is also clearly having a good time but, with his rather unfortunate barrelhouse honky-tonk piano solo, that enjoyment fails to extend to the listener. Lightweight fun overall, and probably more enjoyable than the other lesser cut 'Lay Down Stay Down'.

'Mistreated'. (Blackmore, Coverdale)

A real enduring Purple classic, this poundingly heavy yet deeply soulful blues epic represents one of Coverdale's finest vocal performances, and is in a different universe to Mk II attempts at the blues such as 'Place In Line'. Blackmore is the real architect of the song musically, and it begins with his guitar delivering the simple, mournful heavily reverb-drenched riff with the single bass and drum beat each time making it sound almost like missiles coming in from the blue and detonating around the listener one at a time. With a final crash, the band come in with the lumberingly heavy verse plodding behind Coverdale's astonishing vocal like great dinosaurs roaming the plains. Coverdale sounds utterly convincing here, with a blues-drenched performance of such power that you swear he is in enormous emotional pain. It's the sort of song he was born to sing, and his urgent 'I've been looking for a woman – uh!' gives the impression that the listeners' daughters had better be locked up for their own safety. His woman has left him, he's been sorely mistreated and he's on the prowl like a wounded animal.

There's more though. After delivering a short but beautifully constructed mid-song section, Blackmore takes over after Coverdale's despairing 'I've been losing my mind!' to take the song by the scruff of the neck and deliver a blistering solo as the pace kicks up to double time and the vocal 'ah-ah' backing sweeps it along. Finally it comes to an end as the track is concluded on Coverdale's final, despairing 'I've been losing my mind' refrain, complete with a shuddering sigh which appears to drain what is left of his soul. It's absolutely top-drawer stuff, and would go on to be played live not only by Purple but also Rainbow, Dio, Whitesnake and Glenn Hughes in their own shows. It seemed everyone wanted a piece of the track, and no wonder – but it has to be said that no-one, no matter how talented a singer, could deliver this like David Coverdale. It is *his* song vocally, and he simply owns it. Interestingly, there was one moment of notable friction when, after spending all night lovingly crafting the vocal harmonies for the closing passage, Coverdale and Hughes were aghast to see Blackmore come in the next morning, declare the vocals to be overpowering the guitar, and have them summarily reduced significantly in volume. Although Coverdale later admitted that it was a correct decision, he says that he was devastated at the time.

'A 200'. (Blackmore, Lord, Paice)

How to follow 'Mistreated' then? Well, wisely (following that vocal tour de force) with an instrumental. Opening with a nice guitar/keyboard riff with a slightly futuristic, 'Dr Who' feel, driven by again by the superlative Paice's martial, insistent drumbeat. Just as it seems it might be running out of steam, enter Blackmore at the two and a half minute mark to deliver a stinging solo taking us through to the end of this four minute track, with some Wakeman-esque Lord work to carry the last 30 seconds or so. It's the perfect way to sign off after the heavy drama of 'Mistreated', and works extremely well.

Oh, and the title? Well, as it turns out 'A 200' was a popular brand of cream used to treat pubic 'infestations', shall we say – and presumably something which had been encountered on the road in certain circumstances. A strange title to use for sure, but one that was just vague enough to be a little intriguing at the time.

Related Songs.

'Coronarias Redig'. (Blackmore, Lord, Paice)
Recorded at the time but not used for the album, this instrumental track was used as the B-Side to the 'Burn' single in the US and 'Might Just Take Your Life' in the UK. There were intended lyrics rumoured but never confirmed (allegedly Coverdale's voice was in a poor state after some overindulgence), which would perhaps go some way to explaining the odd title. Other rumours have it that the name was suggested by Ian Paice, but as to what it actually means there have only been theories. Whatever the answer, the track simply crackles with energy: Blackmore's guitar work has hints of his later 'Catch The Rainbow', and Jon Lord is on similar bullish form. As a throwaway track, this is another joining 'When A Blind Man Cries' and 'Painted Horse' on the 'one that got away' list!

Stormbringer.

Personnel:
David Coverdale: vocals
Ritchie Blackmore: guitars
Jon Lord: keyboards
Glenn Hughes: bass guitar, vocals
Ian Paice: drums and percussion
Record Label: Purple Records (UK), Warners (US)
Recorded August / September 1974, produced by Deep Purple.
Release date: November 1974.
Highest chart places: UK: 6, USA: 20
Running time: 36:31

Album Facts.

For the follow-up to *Burn*, the band headed off to Musicland studios in Germany in August 1974, and by the end of the month they had most of the album in the can. A little more recording was done just before the mixing stage in September, at the Record Plant in Los Angeles. There were problems brewing even before recording began, with Ritchie Blackmore going through a divorce at the time and not even remotely as focused on the record as he could have been. A result of this is that more of the writing was spread around the band, with Hughes in particular bringing overt soul and funk influences in on some tracks, and also when the blues direction which Blackmore had championed cropped up, it was in much more sedate fashion to the blitzkrieg 'Mistreated' approach. As a result of this, Blackmore left the band after the subsequent tour (delivering a famously withering condemnation of the funky material as 'shoe-shine music'), with an eye on forming Rainbow – of which more later.

Another bone of contention for Blackmore was the song 'Black Sheep Of The Family', originally recorded by the band Quatermass in 1970 and featuring his old Outlaws bandmate Mick Underwood on drums. He was very keen to record a cover version of the song, but the rest of the band were against the idea, and vetoed the suggestion. Stung and frustrated by this, Blackmore began harbouring plans to record the song as soon as he had his own project together. Despite all of the criticisms levelled at the album, it contains some excellent material and, while patchy, has truly stellar high points. Interestingly, the album's nine songs make this the greatest number of tracks on any Purple album to this date, despite the relatively brief running time of under 37 minutes – no lengthy epics here!

Album Cover.

The painting which graced the spectacular front cover design was by Joe Garrett, and designed by his company Joe Garrett Design along with John Coletta. It is based on an iconic 1927 photograph of a tornado, taken by Lucille

Handberg in Minnesota. It had already been adapted for use as part of the cover painting adorning the 1970 Miles Davis album *Bitches Brew*, while it was later used in its original untouched form for the 1986 Siouxsie And The Banshees album *Tinderbox*. For the *Stormbringer* cover the basis of the picture is kept intact, with the farm building in the field where it should be, although it is given a new and extremely dramatic stormy sky. Added to the picture was the small matter of a flying horse riding the clouds with rainbow lightning coming from its wings. The effect was eyecatching to say the least, and as a front cover image it must surely rank as Purple's best. The US cover was given a bluer tint than the UK edition, the reasons for which are unclear. Opinions over which is better vary, though I would go for the UK version. There was also, notably, a specially designed band name logo done for the cover – whereas previous albums, other than the hand-drawn *Book Of Taliesyn*, had merely shown the band name in plain typeface, even when the album title had its own logo (*Fireball, Burn* etc), this time the reverse is true, with the album title in plain lettering instead. The effect is striking.

There was a different story beyond the front cover, however, with one of the biggest wastes of cover artwork potential in the whole of rock music, as the album was not given a gatefold sleeve treatment, so that the wraparound effect of the cover, which continues over the two panels, was wasted. Worse still, the lyrics, while included this time out, were printed on the rear cover in the absence of any insert, so that the effect of the back cover section of the picture was ruined – and to make matters worse the white typeface used made some of the words barely legible. It is hard to work out who would have sanctioned this, as the addition of a simple gatefold would have allowed the magnificent spread to flourish, while the lyrics could have gone on the inner gatefold. However, such was the way of it. A gatefold cover was finally produced decades later for a double vinyl 35th Anniversary edition, which was beautifully done. Time had at last, if belatedly, done justice to the artwork.

'Stormbringer'. (Blackmore, Coverdale)

If the title track was a major statement of intent on *Burn*, so it also is here, with 'Stormbringer', well, 'storming' out of the traps in tremendous style. An opening salvo of juddering power chords and spiralling keyboard fanfares gives way to a dark, brooding and powerful Blackmore riff which is as heavy as anything the band have ever come up with. It's an absolutely stupendous opening, and ranks along with such classic Purple intros as 'Speed King', 'Highway Star' and 'Fireball' in its effectiveness. Coverdale's lyric (once again written at Blackmore's request in the same fantasy vein as 'Burn') may be a long way from his regular comfort zone, but it contains some of the best heavy metal couplets you'll ever find ('Rainbow shaker on a stallion twister / Bareback rider on the eye of the sky' – brilliant!) – at the time of Coverdale's own *Purple Album* decades later he insisted that 'Stormbringer' was a heavy metal song. I know, because I wrote the bloody thing!' Blackmore's splendid solo on the track foreshadows the even greater song on his own later masterpiece 'Stargazer', and can clearly be seen as containing the seeds of that monumental work.

Like *Burn* before it, Coverdale's vocal performance here (Hughes is only featured on harmony vocals in the chorus) shows just how well he could carry off the Purple job when he was on his best form and the material was right – he is scintillating here. Note that, at the very start of the song when the main riff first comes in, there is some indistinct backwards vocal from Coverdale. Many have speculated on this over the years, with the most common claim being that he is growling 'C**ksucker, mother**ker, Stormbringer', but Hughes has gone on record as claiming that he was actually reciting lines uttered in the film *The Exorcist* by Linda Blair, when she encounters the priest. Also refuted is the widely held claim that the song is referencing Michael Moorcock's writing, and the 'demon sword' Stormbringer wielded by his heroic character Elric. Coverdale actually insists that he was not familiar with Moorcock's books until after the album was recorded, when he came across some on his return to England. Indeed, the song does not appear to reference a sword, demonic or otherwise, and this explanation seems likely, although it could conceivably have inspired the title.

'Love Don't Mean A Thing'. (Blackmore, Coverdale, Hughes, Lord, Paice)

As a complete contrast to 'Stormbringer' comes this slow, swampy, funky blues track, which is the first sign that there might be a wind of change blowing through this album, quite apart from the one on the cover. A nice, if throwaway, lyric about needing money above such trifles as romance, is delivered superbly by, mainly, Coverdale – once again showing that his voice simply dripped blues and soul. Hughes is less impressive on this one, electing to show his vocal range with 'gymnastics' that if anything detract from the bluesy intent of the song. Blackmore, perhaps surprisingly considering his oft-voiced disapproval of this type of direction the band were beginning to follow, plays some beautifully subtle yet effective guitar on this, elevating it significantly. It may not be a track often mentioned in people's lists of favourites, but it's a good one nonetheless.

'Holy Man'. (Coverdale, Hughes, Lord)

'Holy Man' is a song primarily associated with Glenn Hughes, as it is the only track on the album to feature his vocal only, but in interviews with the author both he and Coverdale have revealed that they both had a lot of input into it, with the latter expanding this to state that he 'wrote a lot of that song back in the day. I wrote the verse vocal and the riff, because I remember Jon and Ian saying "there's no way on earth you're going to get Ritchie to play that riff", whereas he never batted an eye, actually. Glenn did the chorus lyric, and Jon came up with the synthesizer pattern'. Hughes concurs, in fact stating that 'David and I wrote the majority of that song ourselves, and Jon came in towards the end and added some parts to it'. It has been speculated that 'Called to Madonna, to give me a line' was some reference to the cocaine habit which was starting to get a grip on Hughes at this time, but he absolutely refutes this. ''Holy Man' was actually written about the endurance of being on the road, and having to find inner strength to cope with things. It's calling to Madonna to give me some help, or advice, that's what it is. It was never, ever about cocaine, because while I may have taken drugs one thing I never ever did was to glamourise it in a lyric. It was a song about spiritual support and strength, basically'.

It's certainly an excellent song, and possibly Hughes' best vocal performance on a Purple track, He tackles it in a more straightforward, simple vocal style and it really shines, with some lines delivered with such clarity that you realise just what a gifted singer he really is. Blackmore also, as alluded to by Coverdale above, excels on the song, playing some beautifully sympathetic, bluesy lines to embellish the verses and cutting loose a little more on the heavier chorus. This is one of those songs which rarely gets its due yet really emphasises the quality apparent on this often misunderstood album. It's a small gem. Significantly, it is the first song on a Purple studio album since 'Chasing Shadows' and 'Blind' on the third album, not to include Blackmore in the writing credits.

'Hold On'. (Coverdale, Hughes, Lord, Paice)

If the previous tracks still indicated a band pulling in roughly the same direction, this one marked the first real divisive indications, with all four members except Blackmore being credited this time. Indeed, our outspoken guitarist made no secret of his dislike for the track, even claiming in one interview that he was so disinterested that he played the guitar solo using just his thumb, though this does seem doubtful when listening to it, from a purely physical point of view. In point of fact, until that solo comes in shortly after the two minute mark there is very little guitar present at all on this agreeably funky shuffle. Coverdale and Hughes alternate verses to pretty good effect, and there are nice harmony vocals in the chorus. Blackmore's solo, be it fingers, thumbs or toes, is well constructed but does give the impression that he is dashing it off 'by the numbers', in a reported single take. A nice, infectious little track, it nonetheless runs out of steam some time before the end of its five minute duration. One thing is certain, you were never going to see the band playing this kind of thing live.

'Lady Double Dealer'. (Blackmore, Coverdale)

Another Blackmore / Coverdale collaboration, and apart from 'Stormbringer' the only other outright rocker on the album. Much faster paced, it relies on its speed and groove more than the ominous, gothic heaviness of the title track – but is none the worse for it. The opening riff seems as if the song might lack a little bite, but the great moment when Coverdale's heavily echoed voice enters with 'Get out of my way, I'm getting tired of you' all is saved. A great vocal performance again from the hugely impressive frontman, and Blackmore's guitar solo is as far away from his lacklustre turn in 'Hold On' as you could wish to get. He sounds like his old energised self as he wrings tortured vibrato out of his Strat, and it does beg the question as to whether he was exorcising some of his frustrations – be they band or personal – in the process. There is an oddly Beatles-like middle eight inserted into proceedings, which shouldn't work yet somehow does, with Hughes taking this part well (barring an interjected 'ooh baby' which does not sit completely with the overall bitterness and invective of the lyric). It is no surprise that this was one of only three tracks to make it into the live set.

'You Can't Do It Right (With The One You Love)'. (Blackmore, Coverdale, Hughes)

The most flat-out funky track on the album, this is another divisive track among fans. Very much a Hughes piece, he has admitted to being a massive Stevie Wonder fan, especially around the time of this album, and boy does it show here. Jon Lord's funk-driven keyboard riff sounds very much like a clavinet, and very reminiscent of Wonder's classic 'Superstition'. Coverdale and Hughes trade vocals here, and do it well, and as a commercial funk-soul song it is a decent enough one, but the fact that it made no concession at all to rock, not even in the token way that 'Hold On', for example, did, was a bridge too far for some long-term Purple fans, who used this track in particular as a stick with which to beat the album. A brave move, for sure, but whether it belonged on a Deep Purple album is a debate which can still cause heated disagreement. As an aside, it is interesting to hear a forebear of Joe Walsh's similar – though rocked-up – 'Life In The Fast Lane' here.

'High Ball Shooter'. (Blackmore, Coverdale, Hughes, Lord, Paice)

A more rock 'n' roll offering here for sure, but it has to be said not a particularly noteworthy one. A paean to the humble groupie, a dull, plodding riff underpins a simplistic boogie, with some of the worst lyrics ever to grace a Deep Purple song – even counting some of the horrors Gillan had visited upon us. Lines such as 'Now I wanna play a piano / But my fingers don't agree' and, even worse, the chorus of 'High ball shooter, you sure ripped the low ones off me' are really quite inexcusable. Paice does his best to save this with an energetic performance, but it's too little, too late for the task at hand. Thankfully, two much, much better songs were to come along to close the album.

'The Gypsy' . (Blackmore, Coverdale, Hughes, Lord, Paice)

The only song apart from the title track and 'Lady Double Dealer' to make the live set, and it is easy to see why, as this is a truly superb song, and a world away from the preceding banality of 'High Ball Shooter.' Opening with a strident, ominous yet beautiful guitar riff, it is immediately ear-catching, and leads into two verses sung in near-perfect harmony by Coverdale and Hughes. When this part of the song finishes after a couple of minutes, with half of the track to go, it seems as if we must have either a lyrical reprise or some sort of development musically – but part of the genius here is that, somehow, we don't. It does morph into a short but mysterious Blackmore solo, perfectly understated, but other than that the main riff is simply repeated, altered, taken up and down in pitch and generally allowed to pull the listener into its hypnotic orbit. Some tremendously placed rolls from the continually underrated Paice lift things just subtly enough to another level, and by the time of the fade, you don't want it to stop. The enigmatic lyrics help this recipe as well, with the protagonist going to see the mysterious gypsy of the title, though we learn that not only is his life now 'at an end', but he previously 'came to see you once before, one hundred years ago', begging the speculation as to whether he was some kind of immortal given the gift / curse of mortality, or some other reason. It's thought-provoking, and addictive stuff. One of the very best Purple Mk III songs, but stiff competition was coming up.

'Soldier Of Fortune'. (Blackmore, Coverdale)

The closing track on the album is a song which has become one of the best known Purple tracks of all time, and certainly their most revered ballad. Once again this is a Blackmore / Coverdale collaboration – a pairing which produced three prime tracks on this album, interestingly. A great shame they never worked together again.

In an interview with the author for the Classic Rock Society, David Coverdale spoke revealingly about the writing and recording of the track: 'Ritchie and I came up with that when we were rehearsing at Clearwell Castle, while everybody else was outside playing soccer. When we presented the idea to the guys later, at Musicland, nobody got it; nobody wanted to do it. So Ritchie and I cut a demo of it right there at Musicland, and then they got it, so we recorded it of course. I distinctly remember Ritchie saying at the time, though, "that's the last time I'm doing *that!*" you know, because people didn't trust him to know what was going to be good'. Further on the musical genesis of the track, he continued 'One of the things that Ritchie and I had in common when we started working together was a love for early Jethro Tull, and the thing of incorporating bits of Bach, modal music, English folk music, all that. And 'Soldier Of Fortune' was, I think, the pinnacle of what we did in that sort of vein'. Indeed, he also claimed that Blackmore was initially a little disappointed that he hadn't actually produced literal lyrics about a historical soldier of fortune returning home, but in truth the lyric is magnificent as it is. Without an obvious, clear meaning, the song hits just the right note of regret for things unfulfilled and a sort of wistful nostalgia which can be absolutely heart-wrenching when listened to in the right mood. 'Mistreated' is the only possible rival to this as Coverdale's finest vocal performance in Purple, and even that has a hard time matching the perfect, aching tone achieved here.

Matching the vocals is Blackmore's divine guitar solo. Simple in its construction, every bit of reverb, every little string bend and every bit of timing is perfection, and as the final recorded solo he contributed to the band in the '70s, there could not be a better sign-off. As with 'Mistreated' it has gone on to have another life onstage, with Coverdale performing it many times down the years with Whitesnake – sometimes inserted brilliantly into 'Mistreated', and sometimes unaccompanied, sitting on the front of the stage, but always to brilliant effect – and Blackmore has gone on to revive the track with his Blackmore's Night project, with his wife Candice giving a nice performance in an incredibly difficult pair of shoes to fill.

It was time for the curtain to come down on Ritchie Blackmore's time with Purple, albeit with one last live 'hurrah'.

Made In Europe

Personnel:
David Coverdale: vocals
Ritchie Blackmore: guitars
Jon Lord: keyboards
Glenn Hughes: bass guitar, vocals
Ian Paice: drums and percussion
Record Label: Purple Records (UK), Warners (US)
Recorded 3-7 April 1975, Graz, Saarbrucken and Paris, produced by Deep Purple.
Release date: October 1976
Highest chart places: UK: 12
Running time: 45:47

Album Facts.

Although this Mk III live album was not released until 1976, after the band
had broken up, I include it here, and not after *Come Taste The Band*, as it is
where it logically sits. The material was recorded in April 1975, in Graz, Austria,
Saarbrucken, Germany and Paris, France – the final three dates performed by
that incarnation of the band, and of course Blackmore's – as we thought at the
time – 'last stand'. The album does not credit which recording comes from
which show, but most of the material supposedly comes from the Saarbrucken
gig. It has also been claimed that the crowd noise has been doctored – and
there is a clearly obvious tape loop of the crowd at the end of the album to
support this. Nonetheless, when the album appeared it was eagerly snapped
up as it formed a perfect 'pair' with *Made In Japan*, right down to the similar
title and cover design – though the debate remains about whether it should
have been another double album to match its predecessor, or whether it was
best to put out the single disc so that it snapshots the Mk III material only, as
opposed to duplicating some Mk II tracks from *Japan*.

Album Cover.

The cover to the album is something of a mixed bag in many ways. The actual
design, by Phil Duffy, is actually first-rate, with a superb live shot of the band
in action on the front (albeit with a curiously seated audience) and individual
shots on the back and inside the gatefold. The tracks are listed on the back,
as well as inside, and the main spread of the inner gatefold is a striking photo
of lighter-holding fans (not a regular sight at Purple shows though, it has to
be said! On stage at least, lighter-waving ballads were not exactly their stock
in trade). Where things fall down are the bizarre, and quite hopeless sleeve
notes gracing the inner gatefold. Credited to Geoff Barton and Pete Makowski
of *Sounds* magazine (why it should take two of them for the herculean task of
cobbling together a couple of hundred words, we can only guess), these notes
take up their first half waffling about Evans and Simper, Gillan and Glover,
'Hush', 'Child In Time' and 'Smoke On The Water'. Once they have finished

eulogising about a different line-up, the fact that the album was recorded at the final Mk III shows is finally mentioned, although even then it writes off Mk IV by stating that, in the minds of many fans 'things were never the same', before immediately signing off by saying that here is a chance 'to come taste the band'. 'Confused' isn't the word for it. Actually no, I take that back. 'Confused' is exactly the word for it.

On the plus side, the great band logo used on *Stormbringer* is back here, and taken to a new level with a gorgeous purple and yellow colour scheme. A shame it was never used again on an album (though in later years it was used extensively on the band's merchandising), but it has to be said that they push the boat out this time with it, as all of the track listings appear in the same font, back and inner, and the band line-up on the front! Maybe just a little too much of a good thing. Overall, imperfect as it is, the sleeve does make a nice partnership with *Made In Japan*, as of course was intended.

As a postscript, for an almost uncannily similar front cover design, see the splendidly titled Doobie Brothers album *What Were Once Vices Are Now Habits* from 1974. The similarity is quite evident!

Song-writing credits as per *Burn* and *Stormbringer* albums.

'Burn'.

The track here opens just like 'Speed King' used to, with an opening 30-second salvo of pure noise, before Blackmore takes it up with 20 seconds of delicately picked guitar, whereupon Coverdale steps up to the mike to mutter, almost under his breath 'Rock and roll...' and the riff slams in. A fantastic moment, and certainly one of the great live album openings. The version of the track following is possibly even better than the studio version, with Paice in absolutely thunderous form, while Blackmore is on fire – it would appear that he wanted to pull out all the stops for his final appearances, and so it proved. His solo is inspired, with Lord also on imperious form. There have been a lot of claims that Hughes re-recorded some of his vocals which were dubbed on afterwards, but in truth it's not really relevant. This is Deep Purple at their absolute fire-engine best.

'Mistreated' (interpolating 'Rock Me Baby').

Ah, the track which introduced the word 'interpolating' to the vocabulary of a million teenagers in 1976. In contrast to 'extrapolating', it was hardly a commonly used word, let's face it. 'Rock Me Baby' is actually an old blues song, written by BB King with Joe Josea, but it's not especially crucial to the track.

In truth, while there are transcendent moments (such as when the band come in on five and a half minutes), and Blackmore is on great form, it's a rambling and unfocused version. The great moments are frustratingly broken up by noodling guitar and interminable cries of 'Baby baby baby!' from Coverdale. The cunningly interpolated 'Rock Me Baby' is little more than a snippet of the original, and if you blinked you could almost miss it. It could have easily been edited out, as indeed, at almost twelve minutes, so could some more of the track.

On the plus side, it is the first recorded instance of David Coverdale's trademark 'Here's a song for ya!' introduction, which is always nice and familiar to hear.

'Lady Double Dealer'.

Another high energy version here, with the studio version definitely improved upon. The tremendous echo effect on Coverdale's voice is replicated extremely well, Blackmore's solo is full of passion, and the song is generally much higher-octane than the studio version. The mid-section ('I gave love to you...'), originally by Hughes alone, is here sung in harmony by the two, and works well for it. Great rendition, four minutes, in and out, no filler. A contrast to 'Mistreated', and even more so to what comes next...

'You Fool No One'.

Sixteen minutes and forty two seconds. Yes, that's almost seventeen minutes taken up with a track which originally came in at under five. It's clear that we're into the sometimes genius, sometimes painful, 'Deep Purple Extended Version' territory again. So, which is it this time?

Well, as you might expect it's a bit of a mixture of the two, but it doesn't lean towards the positive. There are some powerful bits here, undeniably – but they are too few and too far between, and mostly provided by Ritchie Blackmore. For a start the song proper takes around four minutes to get going, which is not far off the total length of the studio version. That gives a clue to how things will develop. In actual fact, it you were to remove all of the extraneous soloing, you would be left with around five minutes of the song. Elsewhere, you get riffs thrown in like 'Hava Nagila' and 'Wild Thing' (perhaps it should have been 'Interpolating Wild Thing'?) Despite his excellent playing elsewhere on the track, Blackmore's unaccompanied showcase is interminable, with the feeble blues section in particular everything that 'Mistreated' isn't. After this, the band go back into the song again, but the listener's fears are of course realised when, a single verse later, in comes the drum solo.

The main riff itself is – much more apparently than the studio version – very similar to the treatment Rainbow would give to the Yardbirds classic 'Still I'm Sad', and Blackmore even slips a little quote from that song's melody into his first solo, so there may have been a little 'inspiration' going on there. Not sixteen minutes which repay repeated listening – how this got the nod over the also-played 'The Gypsy' is a mystery on a par with 'Black Night' being omitted from *Made In Japan*.

'Stormbringer'.

Fortunately, after the excesses just served up, the palate is cleansed by this straight-up rocking delivery of 'Stormbringer'. It's a good, heavy version, though Lord's solo is perhaps not his most effective. Certainly a great way to close the album, but I would still give a slight nod to the studio version this time, though it is a close thing. If nothing else, the track is notable for Coverdale's extraordinary intro, where he seemingly almost strips the paint from the walls with his 'This is a song from our last album ... a song called ... STORMBRINGER!!!'

And with that, Deep Purple Mk III are gone.

Come Taste The Band.

Personnel:
David Coverdale: vocals
Tommy Bolin: guitar, vocals
Jon Lord: keyboards
Glenn Hughes: bass guitar, vocals
Ian Paice: drums and percussion
Record Label: Purple Records (UK), Warners (US)
Recorded August 1975, produced by Martin Birch and Deep Purple.
Release date: October 1975.
Highest chart places: UK: 19, USA: 43
Running time: 37:16

Album Facts.

With Blackmore finally gone to pastures new, it was decision time for the remaining 'Purple People'. Straight away they elected to carry on, and brought in young American hot-shot guitarist, Tommy Bolin, previously with The James Gang, who had impressed Coverdale in particular with his playing on the Billy Cobham album *Spectrum*. It was a brave choice, as Bolin was anything but a straight hard rock player, and with his funk and jazz-rock inclinations there was a clear intention not to make any kind of U-turn from the developing Purple sound. In fact, however, the resulting *Come Taste The Band* album has, overall, a much more hard rock focus than *Stormbringer*, and got the balance between the rock and the newer influences just about right. Glenn Hughes was in the grip of much-publicised substance abuse at the time (primarily cocaine), and was sent home shortly before the end of recording in order to hopefully clean up a little before touring commenced, but what nobody realised at this time was the extent of Bolin's own problems, this time with heroin. What nobody could foresee when the album was recorded was the extent that these demons would overtake him on the subsequent tour, and ultimately take his life only a year later. The band actually imploded following the last of four British shows in March 1976 at Liverpool Empire (a show attended by the author, as a teenager)! For now though, there was a strong album and a seemingly bright future for Deep Purple Mk IV...

Album Cover.

Strangely, it was back to the deluxe gatefold treatment now, after the previous two studio albums, and quite a classy one it was too. Designed by Castle, Chappell & Partners, the front cover showed a brandy glass, full, with the band members' faces superimposed inside of it and the album title inscribed upon it in elegant lettering, as if from an invitation. The reverse showed the same glass, empty and without the band, with a prominent lipstick mark on the rim. Inside the laminated gatefold were five photos of the band members, with a collage of lots of live and candid shots below the relevant members (confusingly, Hughes is pictured with an acoustic guitar, surely leading some more casual listeners to assume it was in fact Bolin). The credits were above this. There was lots to look at, and some great photos, though as usual with Purple it was all monochrome. A pattern really was forming by this time in that regard.

There was also an inner sleeve with the lyrics provided. Why *Stormbringer* couldn't have been afforded this treatment is a seemingly unanswerable question. There could be the fact that the record company wanted to give all the profile they could to boost the new line-up, but by that same token *Burn* had been given the same 'no gatefold, no insert' treatment when Mk III launched, so we are no clearer.

'Coming Home'. (Coverdale, Paice, Bolin)

The opening song on the album, yet the last to be recorded, when the band realised they needed one more track to complete the record, this is actually a storming opener, setting things off at a blistering pace. As Coverdale said in an interview with the author, after revisiting the track for his *Purple Album* project, 'That song, actually, was written right at the end of recording *Come Taste The Band*, literally on the last day. We'd discovered we were a few minutes short for the album, and we couldn't have a fifteen minute side, so Tommy Bolin and myself went off and wrote it in the studio. I just rediscovered recently that Paicey's there on the credits – I dunno what he did, apart from play the drums! Anyway, it's still got that hundred miles an hour tempo, that's still intact. It's still like a Tobacco Auction trying to sing the bloody thing!'

The lyrics are a typical album-starting, rock-and-roll celebrating sort of affair, and as such work pretty well, with the opening 'My mama showed me how to rock in the cradle, but I learned how to roll along' having the spirit of 'Good Golly said little Miss Molly' way back on 'Speed King'. There is a little chuckle to be had at the line 'Grooving to American Bandstand, BB on stage with Lucille', as it was very unlikely that anyone in the North East of England was 'grooving' to anything like American Bandstand at that time. Still, in the same way that English towns and counties don't lend themselves to songs like their American counterparts, 'Grooving to Top Of The Pops' wouldn't really have worked.

For Bolin's part, he immediately stamps his very different style on proceedings, and the 'wall of noise' intro trick leading into a spiralling keyboard and then into the galloping riff is an inspired opening. Lord shifts between Hawkwind-esque keyboard sounds and pounding piano. The backing vocals here are Bolin, as indeed is the bass on the track, as Hughes had already left the sessions. Overall, this is heavy, insistent, powerful and it *rocks*. Oddly, it was rarely played live – only a handful of times in America, by all accounts, which is very strange for a track which sounds tailor made for the stage. Still, refer back to 'Fireball', 'Woman From Tokyo' etc, and perhaps we shouldn't be so surprised.

'Lady Luck'. (Cook, Coverdale)

This strutting, cocksure track has an interesting origin. Credited to Cook / Coverdale, many fans at the time were intrigued as to who the unknown 'Cook' might be (the only clue in the sleeve notes was a different publisher for the track). In actual fact, it referred to Jeff Cook, who had been the singer in an old band of Bolin's called Energy. They never released a studio album, but there is live recorded evidence of the band, which includes them playing this very track. Bolin played the song to Purple, and they were keen to record it. However, he was unable to remember all of the words, so Coverdale wrote a new lyric for it and it was released with the agreement of Cook, who gave the band his blessing, as indeed one would expect him to, given the likely royalties to be accrued. In Coverdale's hands, it becomes another tale of a shady, mysterious woman, but as he often did back then he threw some neat phrases into the mix to make it sound good -'She was a jukebox dancer, a blue-eyed gypsy queen' and, best of all, 'A feathercane Lady Midnight'. He did have a way with words, no doubt. The new lyrics may not be Shakespeare, but they fit the swaggering tone of the music perfectly. A perfect groove for a live setting, this one did make it as a setlist regular.

'Getting Tighter'. (Bolin, Hughes)

A collaboration between Bolin and Hughes only, if ever there was a song which perfects the mix of rock and funk in a way that *Stormbringer* only tried to do, this is it. A whiplash Bolin riff manages to be heavy and yet funky as hell at the same time, which is some trick. Audiences didn't know whether to dance or headbang to this one! Midway through, there is a pure funk break courtesy of Hughes, which can be jarring when it comes in yet leads back into the main body of the song well. Both men are at the peak of their powers here as Hughes takes the lead vocal with some gusto.

There has been much speculation down the years as to whether the lyrics refer to getting 'tight' as in 'drunk', and referring to Hughes' issues at the time, but he refutes this. In a recent interview with the author he stated 'Absolutely not. To me, and this was what was in my mind when I wrote the song, 'Getting Tighter' was about "how good can this groove get, how tight am I with that bass drum" – it's about how tight the music can be, and getting as great a groove as we possibly could. It was a celebration of that, really, "We're tight, we're grooving, we're ready to go to a club, let's go"'. Unsurprisingly the track took up permanent residence in the live shows, generally in an extended format with the sort of instrumental interplay you might expect it to have.

'Dealer'. (Bolin, Coverdale)

This is one of four Bolin / Coverdale co-writes on the album – reflecting the massive influence that Bolin actually had on the material. He is actually the chief musical contributor on seven of the ten tracks, which is astonishing considering his debutant status, and a testimony to just how gifted he was when firing on all cylinders. A snake-hipped bluesy riff from Bolin drives the song along, with his guitar exhibiting an absolutely filthy, raw, dirty tone that is perfect for the subject matter concerning, well, a drug dealer of course. This track bears a strong resemblance to the sort of thing Coverdale would go on to do with the early incarnations of Whitesnake, while Bolin's extended guitar workout is magnificent. If they had gone on to reproduce this sort of performance in the live arena on a regular basis, they could have laid the 'Blackmore Ghost' to rest, but unfortunately history doesn't show that, and tends to record this album as little more than a footnote. The song was played live, but infrequently, sadly. Bolin also takes a rare lead vocal toward the end of this song ('In the beginning all you wanted...')

'I Need Love'. (Bolin, Coverdale)

Another quite funky track, it grooves along nicely in a sort of funked-up Bad Company vein for most of its duration, before it dissolves into another rather incongruous pure funk breakdown midway through, and from that point on never seems to fully regain its swagger. The lyrics are a rather standard tale of 'Woman Leaves Coverdale – Coverdale Misses Woman – Coverdale Needs Someone To Satisfy His Urges'. It made the setlist for the 1975 Asian dates but was dropped by the time the band wound their weary way into 1976. It's not the album's finest moment.

'Drifter'. (Bolin, Coverdale)

Side two of the vinyl opens with Coverdale finding himself in his default state when not yearning after the charms of a devilish female, namely a 'ramblin' man', 'on the road to nowhere'. Happily, however, it seems that, while he was of course 'born a loser', he is also 'beyond the law', which must come in handy. To be fair this is a pretty good track, with a snaking, mid-paced swagger replaced, briefly in the chorus and then for an extended ending, with the kind of double tempo boogie that Purple simply didn't do enough of by this point. It did make the live repertoire but, like other tracks, it was dispensed with when the setlist was cut down after the Asian leg.

'Love Child' (Bolin, Coverdale)

A great, ringing guitar riff from Bolin soars above the band for this tale of Coverdale, unsurprisingly, being driven to distraction by another temptress. It drives the verses along as a grindingly heavy rock track before edging into slightly more funked up territory for the chorus. The funk is extended with Lord delivering an uncharacteristically – well, there is no other way to put this – 'funky' solo. Just as it begins to outstay its welcome however, that great riff comes chiming in again and the band grind to a powerful climax. This one stayed in the setlist until the final UK shows.

'This Time Around / Owed To 'G''. (Hughes, Lord, Bolin)

Two tracks which were sequenced as a single cut on the album, and always played together in the live shows, where they stayed until the end. 'This Time Around' is a soulful ballad sung with heartfelt earnestness by Hughes, and despite Lord playing all of the instruments on the track (according to the album credits), it is clearly his 'baby', as it were. In a recent interview with the author he explained about the lyrics: 'What happened there was that the very same week I wrote that song I found myself getting a bit deeper into trouble with the drink and too many drugs, and all those problems, and I was beginning to think "What if this is the end", you know. So I was kind of writing about that, being on the edge, with the world hanging in doubt, but trying to bring some love into it. I was in a pretty dark place then'. This does make sense when looking into the words, which are a little more obscure and elusive than the average soul ballad.

The track morphs straight into Bolin's upbeat instrumental 'Owed To G' with a few steady introductory beats from Paice, and it's a great track on its own merit. A sprightly guitar-led instrumental piece with its head in the clouds and its feel anchored in a solid rock beat, it's one of the best things on the album. Hughes has gone on to explain that the G of the title is nothing to do with the musical key, but in fact refers to George Gershwin.

'You Keep On Moving'. (Coverdale, Hughes)

The only Coverdale / Hughes songwriting collaboration in the Purple repertoire, amazingly, this track was actually written as early as 1973, shortly after Coverdale joined the ranks. As Hughes explained in the aforementioned interview 'Yes, that was written by David and I above a Wimpy Bar in Saltburn-on-Sea, which is where he was living at the time, in August of 1973. But Ritchie Blackmore, bless him, didn't like 'You Keep On Moving', so we had to wait until Tommy came in before we could use it. I love it, it's one of my favourites, for sure'.

Indeed, once again, it is hard to grasp Blackmore's dislike of the song, as it is a superb piece, from the ominous, quiet introduction through to the huge heavy arrival of the band ('Everyday... wheels are turning'), with Bolin again providing some brilliant guitar, not least his exultant, ringing line over the 'and the cry, still returning' line. It might have taken some time, but the song was finally, deservedly used, and quite fittingly brought down the '70s Purple curtain, at least in the studio. Released as a single without success - an odd choice as it is not the most commercial track on the album - the song was played live, but was dropped after a while, unfortunately.

Now it was time to see what Mr Blackmore had in his locker to come back with...

Ritchie Blackmore's Rainbow

Personnel:
Ritchie Blackmore: guitar
Ronnie James Dio: vocals
Mickey Lee Soule: keyboards
Craig Gruber: bass
Gary Driscoll: drums

Record Label: Oyster (UK), Polydor (US)
Recorded February / March 1975, produced by Martin Birch, Ritchie Blackmore
and Ronnie James Dio.
Release date: August 1975.
Highest chart places: UK: 11, USA: 30
Running time: 36:54

Album Facts.

As early as January 1975, while still touring with Purple, Ritchie Blackmore
began hatching plans to record some solo material – he knew he was going
to leave Purple after the tour ended, even though, in true Purple tradition,
the rest of the band were in the dark about it. Honestly, such was the shroud
of secrecy and deception around every line-up change the band had, it's a
wonder that an ex-member never turned up at a gig, like the famed Japanese
soldier who didn't know the war had ended some twenty or thirty years
later! Maybe that's where Rod Evans is now...

Anyhow, needing a band to play on this two-song session, Blackmore was
speaking with Ronnie James Dio, whose band Elf had supported Purple on
many occasions, and whose vocal style he admired very much. A plan was
hatched (there we are again) to poach the members of Elf and rebrand them
as his 'instant backing group' – with the notable exception of poor old Steve
Edwards, the guitarist with Elf at the time, who was obviously surplus to
requirements and was dropped. The first song planned for the session was
the track he'd wanted to record with Purple, 'Black Sheep Of The Family',
and as the intended B-side of the single he had the music for what would
become 'Sixteenth Century Greensleeves', for which he asked Dio to write
lyrics. Cellist Hugh McDowell, from ELO, also played on these first two tracks
– he was helping Blackmore to learn the rudiments of the cello at this time.

The sessions, again at Musicland in Munich, soon turned into a full album,
and recording was finished by March, by which time the other Purple
members still had no idea about his decision to leave. Indeed, the Musicland
studio was in the basement of a Munich hotel, where he was to meet up
with Coverdale and Paice to set off for the tour. This they duly did, with the
Purple pair still oblivious to the fact that he had just recorded his debut solo
album there.

The album was at least held up for release until August 1975, by which time his ties with Purple had been well and truly severed. By that time, however, this line-up, which never played a single gig, had splintered, with Blackmore firing both Gruber and Driscoll during rehearsals for live shows, with Soule then resigning fearing his name was on the next bullet. For now, it was a Blackmore and Dio double act.

The album originally appeared on the Oyster label, with a label picture of a pearl and oyster. Blackmore refused to have it come out on Purple Records, but as he was still under contract, Oyster was created as a subsidiary company. As soon as his contract expired, Polydor bought out Oyster, and subsequent releases of the album appeared first on a red Oyster label, resembling Polydor, and then on Polydor itself.

Album Cover.

The album cover painting, by David Willardson, is simply stunning. A lavish gatefold painting of a mist (or cloud)-shrouded 'guitar castle', complete with Rainbow behind, was the most eye-catching cover illustration of any Purple project to date – nudging out *Stormbringer* by virtue of the laminated gatefold. The crescent moon and the castle supposedly represent the two great influences on Blackmore's writing on the album – the middle east and medieval Europe. The rear cover had the lyrics to Sixteenth Century Greensleeves alone, and also the track listing. Inside the gatefold was a photo spread (monochrome naturally – some things never changed) with one panel taken up by a single, excellent, photo of Blackmore on stage with Purple (no other members are visible), plus the album credits. The other panel has a fairly large portrait shot of Dio, a small band photo and live shots of all the band members (all pictured, of course, with Elf and Purple). It seems a little odd that, for a band destined not to play any live shows, there should be such an emphasis on live photographs. All in all, it is a great cover though. The album was credited to 'Ritchie Blackmore's Rainbow'.

'Man On The Silver Mountain'. (Blackmore, Dio)

Without a doubt, the enduring Rainbow legacy starts here, with one of their most distinctive and recognisable tracks, and one which would go on to be a live staple throughout the band's career. Opening with Blackmore's serpentine, mid-paced guitar riff, the song goes for a hypnotic groove rather than the more frenetic pace it would have in future live workouts. The chorus is lifted by a spiralling guitar line behind Dio's brilliant vocal performance. Dio's fantasy-themed lyrics are a perfect fit both to the music and Blackmore's whole image, and his voice seemed as if it had been destined all along to end up with Ritchie. Timeless. The track was released as a single in October 1975, backed with 'Snake Charmer', but without significant success.

The title is inscribed on Dio's memorial in Hollywood Hills cemetery, Los Angeles. It is a fitting tribute.

'Self Portrait'. (Blackmore, Dio)

A heavy, slow-paced track with immensely dark lyrics by Dio, pleading to be taken away by the devil, seemingly through his painting, it is very much his vocal performance here that lifts the song above the average. Blackmore has described the song as a cross between 'Jesu, Joy Of Men's Desiring' by Bach and 'Manic Depression' by Hendrix, which is certainly a combination to conjure with. The track was only performed live for a short while by the band, though it was revisited a long time later by Blackmore's Night, in an excellent interpretation.

'Black Sheep Of The Family'. (Hammond)

This is the song which, in many ways, was the catalyst for Blackmore's Purple departure, when his wish to record it during the *Stormbringer* sessions was turned down. Originally recorded for the sole album by Quatermass in 1970, it is an entertaining track with much to recommend it, sung in an unusually upbeat fashion by Dio. Ironically, considering the issues with the track, it would have made a perfect fit for the *Stormbringer* album, with its catchy and not-too-heavy rock sound – so who knows what could have perhaps been so easily avoided? Although recorded with the intention of being a single, with 'Sixteenth Century Greensleeves', it was never released as such. Oddly, given his seeming obsession with the track, it never made it into the Rainbow live set!

'Catch The Rainbow'. (Blackmore, Dio)

Side One of the original vinyl closes with this achingly beautiful track, with a chord progression reminiscent at times of 'Soldier Of Fortune', and accompanied by perfectly matched lyrics, which are delivered with immense sensitivity by Dio, who proves here once and for all that he was far from a typical heavy rock vocalist. Blackmore's guitar embroidery throughout this piece is perfect, topped off by one of his most exquisite solos, with a lush keyboard backing. Backing vocals are provided by Shoshana, who was an American operatic singer who had been living with Blackmore around this time. Her real name is Judith Feinstein, but she is not related to ex-Elf member (and Dio's cousin) David Feinstein.

In a radio interview at the time of the album's release, Dio claimed that the song concerned a medieval tale of a stable boy who falls in love with a lady of the court, but their conflicting worlds eventually result in them drifting apart. At six and a half minutes the track is the longest on the album by some distance. It instantly became a live favourite, and was regularly extended to over fifteen minutes in live performance, becoming quite a different beast.

'Snake Charmer'. (Blackmore, Dio)

Opening the second side, this slightly funky, bluesy rocker is something of a lesser track in the context of the album, but the playing is excellent. Unusually,

96

Craig Gruber's bass line drives things to a large extent, with Blackmore providing some distinctly Hendrix-influenced playing over the top. The vocal line is poor, and Dio struggles to make it his own, especially during the lengthy outro which sees him improvising variations on the lyrics – something which he would do to varying degrees of success throughout his career. In fact, with the excellent Blackmore playing going on in the background, it could be argued that this is a track which could have been better served as an instrumental. It was the B-Side to the 'Man On The Silver Mountain' single, and unsurprisingly was never played live.

'Temple Of The King'. (Blackmore, Dio)

One of the most celebrated tracks on the album, 'Temple Of The King' is one of those instances whereby Blackmore's musical vision and Dio's lyrical inspiration were in perfect harmony. The song sounds very medieval-influenced in its structure and instrumentation, with a plaintive guitar figure central to the piece giving is a little bit of a similar feel to 'The Gypsy' from *Stormbringer*. Blackmore himself has claimed that he first got the inspiration for the song while watching a TV programme called *Yoga For Health*.

The lyrical imagery of a rural, peasant people being summoned to the temple, by the mysterious 'great black bell' is perfectly evoked, and a beautifully weeping guitar solo complements it effortlessly. There have been many interpretations of the lyric over the years, ranging from the story of Buddha through to the appearance of 'the year of the Fox' in fantasy literature (there is no oriental year named after the fox), but whatever the actual intent – if indeed there is one – it seems safe to interpret it as a, possibly metaphoric, tale of spiritual searching and destiny. What has been much theorised is that the black bell may represent death, and that the young man of the song may be summoned to take the place of the 'old man', or the king. What is certain is that it is a song of great beauty and elegance, and a standout not only on the album but in Blackmore's career as a whole. This track together with 'Catch The Rainbow' illustrate perfectly where 'The Gypsy' and 'Soldier Of Fortune' were leading.

The song was never played live by Rainbow until the later reformation of the band in the 1990s with the album *Stranger In Us All*, as Blackmore felt it wasn't a piece suitable for the stage.

'If You Don't Like Rock 'n' Roll'. (Blackmore, Dio)

From the sublime to the faintly ridiculous, the gravitas and magic of the previous track is followed up by this rather inconsequential piece of fluff. The band vamp on a twelve-bar rock and roll structure to the accompaniment of Soule's boogie-woogie piano, as Dio relates a banal tale involving a club with loud music playing and a mysterious lady inside the place. The general message seems to be that is necessary to like rock and roll, unsurprisingly. And two and a half minutes later that's it, we're done and there's nothing to see here. They may not have been *entirely* serious on this one, and it is not inconceivable that there was an element of needing a couple of minutes of anything to fill up space. Personally, I'd rather they had simply extended 'Man On The Silver Mountain' or 'Temple Of The King', but such is life. Not played live, except on one single documented occasion as an encore.

'Sixteenth Century Greensleeves' (Blackmore, Dio)

This track from the original 'single session' sees our heroes slap bang back into medieval sword and sorcery fantasy territory again, at least lyrically. Musically this is some way from minstrels and lutes, as the song powers along on a remorseless riff a little reminiscent of Uriah Heep's 'Gypsy'. Blackmore's idea was of a sort of hard rock song with a classical feel, wherein a sort of 'black knight' figure in an old castle is brought to justice. He said that the joint inspiration for both title and subject matter was because he loved the old song 'Greensleeves' (supposedly written by Henry VIII), and he also used to live near Windsor Castle, at which he would often look in order to gain inspiration.

Dio's lyric is a mixed bag on this one. It does itself no favours by opening with the 'Spinal Tap' couplet of 'It's only been an hour, since he locked her in the tower' (which presumably was better than, for example, 'It's only been a bit, since he threw her in the pit'), but he redeems himself with some excellent and powerful 'crossbows in the firelight' imagery. This was another track which went on to become a live fixture, with Blackmore introducing it by playing the original 'Greensleeves'. As stated earlier, Hugh McDowell of ELO plays cello on this.

'Still I'm Sad'. (Samwell-Smith, McCarty)

A strange choice of closing number for the album, this is an instrumental reworking of the old Yardbirds track 'Still I'm Sad', originally found on the B-side of 'Evil Hearted You' in the UK, and of 'I'm A Man' in the US. It also appeared on the dreadfully-titled US album *Having A Rave-Up With The Yardbirds*.

The track begins with a rhythm uncannily similar to 'You Fool No-One', but soon grows beyond that as some magnificently evocative guitar work from Blackmore brings out the marvellously subtle nuances of the melody exceptionally. As it progresses, Shoshana contributes some backing vocals for the second time on the album, but these are low in the mix. It's a great instrumental track for certain, but in future live performance it would get the full vocal performance to superb effect, which does rather beg the question as to why vocals were not added to it here. Perhaps it could have been another contender to be extended and nudge out 'If You Don't Like Rock 'n' Roll', but we'll never know.

Rainbow Rising.

Personnel:
Ritchie Blackmore: guitar
Ronnie James Dio: vocals
Tony Carey: keyboards
Jimmy Bain: bass
Cozy Powell: drums
Record Label: Polydor-Oyster
Recorded February 1976, produced by Martin Birch
Release date: May 1976
Highest chart places: UK: 11, USA: 48
Running time: 33:28

Album Facts.

Generally accepted by the majority of fans as the peak of Rainbow's output, *Rising* appeared in 1976 with an entirely different line-up alongside Blackmore and Dio. Bassist Jimmy Bain was first to arrive, followed by the biggest 'name', Cozy Powell, who had scored three solo singles successes since leaving the Jeff Beck Group earlier in the decade. Keyboard player Tony Carey was last to be drafted in, arriving from a country-rock band. So quickly had the original band been dismantled that this new line-up were already out on tour before the end of 1975.

Three tracks from the album were already written and being performed on that late 1975 tour – namely 'Do You Close Your Eyes', 'Stargazer' and 'A Light In The Black'. Recording was done quickly in Musicland Studios again, in February 1976, in between tours, and as a rule the trio of Blackmore, Bain and Powell would lay down the basic tracks with Carey and Dio adding the keyboards and vocals later.

Album Cover.

For the album cover this time the band went for a similar 'fantasy / rainbow' approach as the debut, but in much more mature style, commissioning a masterpiece of a painting by Ken Kelley, depicting a huge fist grasping a rainbow emerging from a storm-tossed sea, while a small windswept figure on the shore looks on. So classy was this image that it was regularly voted one of the best album covers of the decade in polls of the time. The inner gatefold shows a starkly-lit, serious photo of the band members (in, you guessed it, monochrome), along with the lyrics to 'Stargazer' – which followed the lead of the debut album by including lyrics to only one song – and the credits. The tracklisting appeared on the rear cover alongside five individual live photos of the band.

This time the album was credited to 'Blackmore's Rainbow' – seemingly a halfway-house between the debut title and the simple 'Rainbow' which would appear from the next album onward.

'Tarot Woman'. (Blackmore, Dio)

This opening track, perhaps surprisingly, opens with a lengthy solo keyboard introduction courtesy of Tony Carey – quite a showcase for a new man on a Blackmore record. After this excellent swooping, diving opening, delivered without any of the tortured Hammond-mangling distortion of Jon Lord, the band slowly fade up into the mix before Powell's drums kick the song into full gear at around 1:45. Considering how much Carey's introduction adds to the song, and that Blackmore asked him to come up with it, it does seem odd that he didn't get a writing credit.

The lyrics, according to Dio, tell of visiting a woman who is a Tarot reader, who tells the protagonist to beware of a future relationship, where he will be betrayed, but it is written and delivered in such a fashion that it never, ever sounds like a 'deceitful woman' subject would have in the hands of Gillan or Coverdale – instead it gives more of an epic, mysterious quality to the song. This, straight away, is a band matching Blackmore's vision and enabling him to deliver what he wanted to when leaving Purple. The song structure is quintessentially 'English' hard rock, eschewing any blues inspiration and instead having more in common with Classical music structure. It's a quite brilliant opener, but very surprisingly it was never, ever played live by Rainbow (it *was* done by the much later White Noise project, which saw '90s Rainbow frontman Doogie White link up with members of Mostly Autumn to play – mostly – Rainbow material).

'Run With The Wolf'. (Blackmore, Dio)

In which Dio appears to turn his attention to werewolves and lycanthropy, albeit with more esoteric touches in the form of a break in the ground, hole in the sky and swirling waters. It's all fabulous sounding stuff, and although it's a relatively basic plodding rocker, the trademark uplifting Dio chorus is there to add just the spice it needs. It was never played on stage, but it could have made a great live song.

'Starstruck'. (Blackmore, Dio)

Much simpler lyrical fare here, with this tale of an obsessed stalker that Blackmore had picked up along the way in France. Referring to her as 'Muriel' (this may not be her actual name), he tells how she would be waiting at every airport before he arrived, at every gig and even, he claims, once caught hiding in a bush outside his window. Dio relates this slightly unnerving story with just the right mix of humour and drama, and the music is appropriately playful to match, being quite catchy, with a chorus that, more than anything else on the album, invites the listener to sing along. The song was crying out to be released as a single, but it didn't happen. In fact, no singles were released from the album at all. The track would go on to be played, but only in shortened format, usually as part of the mid-section of 'Man On The Silver Mountain', which rather wasted its potential.

'Do You Close Your Eyes'. (Blackmore, Dio)

If there is a 'filler' track on an album as great as this one (and to be fair, there really shouldn't be when the total running length is under 34 minutes!), this would be the one. Already written as a set-opener on the previous tour, it would go on to be a regular encore song for the duration of Dio's tenure with the band. Of course, 'regular' is not a word which could be used in conjunction with Rainbow encores at this time, as if Blackmore felt the audience, or his performance, did not deserve an encore then he simply would not do one. Indeed, this author recalls a show in Liverpool in 1977 when the band did not return despite sustained demands, and yet at another show at the same venue the next night, they not only obliged with an encore but Blackmore climbed the speaker stacks to reach one of the theatre boxes, damaging the fixtures in the process! You took your chances with the band in those days.

Part of the reason for the song's use as an encore number was to allow Blackmore to improvise extensively, and it would tend to last over ten minutes, which is stretching things a little for a rather run of the mill three minute song. With its rather banal lyric and simplistic good-time rock feel, it was seemingly aiming for a more commercial feel, but on that score it was outdone by 'Starstruck'.

'Stargazer'. (Blackmore, Dio)

Ah, now we are talking! The centrepiece of the album, the song generally regarded as Rainbow's peak, and a track which is never far from the top positions when 'greatest heavy rock song' polls are run. It has been described as 'Ritchie's own 'Stairway To Heaven'', and even the notoriously self-critical, and often dismissive, Blackmore admits is full of merit, even though he has been more scathing of the album as a whole.

Opening with a tremendous Cozy Powell drum break, the song proper hits with immediate power as an epic heavy, rolling riff crashes in. The first verse then leads on to the second riff in the spiralling 'pre-chorus' 'Where was your star' section before the chorus itself releases that accumulated tension with the 'everything more epic than everything else' chorus (In the heat and the rain...'). Rinse, and repeat. Then, just when you think things couldn't get any better (or more 'epic', for that matter), in comes Blackmore's solo, using the Phrygian dominant scale, commonly used in Arabic music, to stunning effect. This solo may be the best constructed and most impressive of his career, as it keeps ramping up and up, causing the hairs on the listener's neck to stand to attention. A final, ringing, descending phrase leads into another Powell drum fill, leading us back into the final verse with redoubled grandeur. This time, however, once the chorus sweeps in, it never stops, carrying on and on as the Munich Philharmonic Orchestra come in with accompaniment. Dio on this occasion brings his ad-lib 'outro' speciality to incredible effect, never putting a foot wrong as he enhances the growing storm of the music again and again. The moment where he sings 'I see a rainbow rising!' is to this day one of the most stunning moments in all of rock music, and his descending line 'I'm coming home', as the strings in turn ascend behind him is similarly jaw dropping. Blackmore admitted that he was inspired by Led Zeppelin's 'Kashmir' when he put the song together and, great as that track is, he outdoes it here. The listener is left breathless and drained by the end of the long, gradual fade-out.

Of course, none of this musical grandeur would have the same effect without Dio's fantastically evocative tale of the wizard using the mass forced labour to build his incredible tower, and his final, climactic fall. It's a perfect marrying of words and music to create something spellbinding. To enhance the orchestra, a keyboard instrument called a Vako Orchestron is used on the track. It is worth noting that there is a 'rough mix' version of the track with another Carey keyboard intro, but it is easy to see why this was dropped as, good as it is in its own right, it creates a very jarring effect when the familiar drum intro comes in, and spoils the effect. The song was written and performed on the 1975 dates before the album, and again on the whole of the following 'Rising' tour, but was dropped after that. In an interview with the author, Ritchie explained that 'You really need an orchestra to build at the end of it. It's a strange song, and working on it from that angle I didn't think it worked so much live. It really needs to build, and whereas on the record you've got the orchestra, on stage you've just got keyboards, and I didn't think it was right.'

'A Light In The Black.' (Blackmore, Dio)

The second lengthy piece, to complete Side Two of the vinyl, is a sort of continuation of the 'Stargazer' story, after the wizard has fallen to his death and the slaves are now free, but, as Dio put it, having lost all sense of purpose until they see the 'light in the black'.

No repeat of that previous song's slow, epic feel though, as this is a hundred miles-per-hour hard rock monster from start to finish. In fact, it has been called 'the birth of power metal', not without some justification. Dio's voice is astonishing on this track, with the echoed long note at the end of each couplet in the verses a stroke of genius. Carey takes the first solo, dancing across the keys over the savage, churning riff behind him, and then, as they bring it up to a crescendo of sorts, Blackmore takes over with an absolute guitar solo masterclass. This is like his iconic 'Highway Star' solo, but possibly even better executed. When the track comes back in, it heads for a breakneck conclusion ending on a power chord as the band 'stop on a dime'. This is the perfect answer to the lengthy fade-out of 'Stargazer', which manages to give the irrational impression that somewhere, they are still playing!

With their contrasting musical magnificence, these two tracks combine to make up possibly the greatest vinyl side of heavy rock music ever recorded. It's *that* good. The song was, like 'Stargazer', written and performed on the 1975 dates before the recording of the album, always as a one-two in succession. It continued to feature on the first dates after the album's release, but was soon dropped, with apparently even the superhuman Cozy Powell struggling with the physical demand of keeping this sort of power-drumming up over ten minutes or so!

On Stage.

Personnel:
Ritchie Blackmore: guitar
Ronnie James Dio: vocals
Tony Carey: keyboards
Jimmy Bain: bass
Cozy Powell: drums
Record Label: Polydor-Oyster
Recorded September and December 1976, produced by Martin Birch
Release date: July 1977
Highest chart places: UK: 7, USA: 65
Running time: 64:11

Album Facts.

Rainbow's only official live release in the 1970s, this double-vinyl album
was recorded in Germany and Japan, in September and December '76, on
the Rising tour. The first thing to note is that 'Stargazer' has been omitted,
which seems a shocking omission, but going by Blackmore's comments
about the problems doing it to his satisfaction on stage, perhaps not
entirely surprising with hindsight. At the time, however, it was greeted
with incredulous disbelief by fans of the *Rising* album. In fact, with 'Do
You Close Your Eyes' not making the cut either, and 'A Light In The Black'
very rarely played by this time, the bizarre situation was that, from a just-
released classic album, the only thing included was a short snatch of
'Starstruck'! To rub these omissions in, the record was very short, averaging
only around 15 minutes per side.

Album Cover.

The album cover was a fairly standard '70s 'live double' cover, consisting
mainly of live photos. The front, which retains the gothic-script band logo
from *Rainbow Rising*, has a band photo with the giant electronically-
controlled rainbow prop above them (it had 4,000 light bulbs and was
controlled by computer – a fairly big deal for '70s technology), against a
stark white border, with the words 'World Tour' around the sides five times
in what were supposed to represent the rainbow colours. They didn't. The
reverse contains the track information and credits (including a lengthy
breakdown of all the band equipment, and details about 'the rainbow'),
while the inner gatefold spread had five individual group shots against
a black backdrop with two 'lights' shining up and out from the centre
bottom. Two inner sleeves contained yet more band shots, on and off the
stage, against a red backdrop. Unless you happen to be fascinated by the
people who helped out on each continent, or precisely what cymbals Cozy
Powell used, there isn't a lot to read.

For the first time, the album is credited to simply 'Rainbow', dropping the names Ritchie or Blackmore. Which was ironic as, since Blackmore was in the process of firing two more members when the album appeared, the 'band dynamic' seemed shaky to say the least!

'Kill The King'. (Blackmore, Dio, Powell)

The album opened, as did the show, with a tape of Judy Garlands's voice from The Wizard Of Oz, saying 'We're not in Kansas any more', and then as her voice echoes away on 'We must be over the Rainbow ... Rainbow ... Rainbow ... Rainbow...' the band crash in with a mighty refrain of the 'Somewhere Over The Rainbow' chorus, morphing straight into the first song proper. It's a tremendous introduction to the show, and worthy of listing as a separate track perhaps.

Nonetheless, the first credited song, which they hurtle straight into, is the as-yet-unreleased breakneck rocker 'Kill The King', a song which was specifically written to open the show, and would not make its studio appearance until 1978, where it opened Side Two of the album *Long Live Rock And Roll*. What a tremendous addition it would have made to *Rainbow Rising*! The first Rainbow track to contain a band credit other than Blackmore and Dio, Cozy Powell got in on the compositional action on this speedy powerhouse, which powers along at a tempo similar to 'A Light In The Black'. The lyrics, talking about nefarious goings on and murderous deeds within a royal family were apparently written with a chess game in mind. Even though the wisdom of writing a new song to open a show with may seem questionable, especially given the paucity of *Rising* material represented, it is undeniably a great opening punch in the face, with the whole band firing on all cylinders.

The track was released as the lead song on a three-track live EP (with 'Man On The Silver Mountain' and 'Mistreated' also shoehorned onto the 7" disc), and it gave the band their first chart success, making it to the dizzy heights of number 44 on the UK singles chart.

Recorded in Munich (intro is Nuremburg).

'Man On The Silver Mountain'. (Blackmore, Dio)

A ten-minute medley format sees this track bookending a rather lame instrumental section with the thrilling title 'Blues' and a short verse-chorus blast of 'Starstruck'. Taken at a faster pace than the original, the song starts off in lively enough fashion but really only hits the stratosphere after the 'Starstruck', when Dio teases the audience with 'You're the man. You're the man. You're the man. You're all ... the ME-EN!!' as the band hurtle back in with a massive burst of power, closing the track on a huge high. The medley format doesn't serve it well, however, and dilutes the impact of both it and 'Starstruck'.

Recorded in Tokyo ('Blues' and 'Starstruck' from a different show to the rest of the track)

'Catch The Rainbow'. (Blackmore, Dio)

Extended to over 15 minutes, this version of the classic ballad turned the delicate original into a tour-de-force of light and shade, with quiet, reflective interludes rubbing shoulders with big, inspired guitar-driven outbursts. The portion of the song before these new improvisational parts is treated the same, with the 'bigger' parts of the original given much more emphasis by the full band. It's a radical reworking, but a successful one, as clearly to attempt to replicate the studio perfection of the original would be impossible. In this way the optimum live potential of the track is realised, and it is an inspired fifteen and a half minutes. It occupied the whole of the original second side of the vinyl.

Recorded in Osaka.

'Mistreated'. (Blackmore, Coverdale)

Introduced a little mischievously by Dio as 'a song that Ritchie wrote' (thus airbrushing Coverdale from history), this lengthy treatment of the Purple classic occupied all of the third vinyl side – though at thirteen minutes, it hardly seems long enough for that privilege. In truth, it's an odd choice of song to add into the set, with Blackmore wanting to forge his own identity away from his Purple past, and with so much Rainbow original material not getting a look in. And in truth, it doesn't entirely work. Blackmore is on good form (though unable to resist the standard lengthy dribble of laid-back bluesy tinkering), but the biggest problem is that the song simply does not fit Dio in any shape or form. Whereas Coverdale used to sound like someone who had something on his mind (and in his pants) that was which was tormenting him beyond endurance, Dio simply sounds as if he is singing a song very well and throwing in all the bluesy clichés he can. When he sings 'I've been mistreated and generally left for dead' it is hard to stifle a wince (or a giggle, depending on your mood). An entertaining enough thirteen minutes, but Lord, how much better it could have been put to use.

Recorded in Cologne.

'Sixteenth Century Greensleeves'. (Blackmore, Dio)

Blackmore prefaces this version with a rendition of the original 'Greensleeves' – though he neglected to give Henry VIII a song-writing credit. It works nicely as an intro, but when the track proper begins it is taken at a thunderously heavy and much faster tempo, making it powerful but also losing some of what made the original great. Some swear by this as the definitive rendition, but I am not quite so sure. It's good though, and excellently done for what it is.

Recorded in Tokyo.

'Still I'm Sad'. (Samwell-Smith, McCarty)

Closing the album, and indeed the Rainbow shows themselves on both this and the 1977 tour, is this full vocal version of the Yardbirds track, recorded as the instrumental closer from the first album. Indeed, the way Dio simply thrives on this melody really makes one wonder why it wasn't done with the vocals in the studio originally. Whereas 'Mistreated' showed him at odds with a song, this is perfectly suited to him, and he makes it his own, wringing every little bit of subtlety and beauty from the melody line, even against the fast-tempo backing of a heavy band accompaniment. His delivery of the line 'my tears just fall into dust!' is an absolute joy. The song is lengthened with some improvisational stuff, with Blackmore even throwing in a snippet of 'God Rest Ye Merry Gentlemen', weaved in so skilfully that it could have come from the same song. Unfortunately, the edit removes the legendary Cozy Powell '1812 Overture' drum solo, which even in audio only was and remains something to behold. Great track to close the album with, nonetheless.

At the very end of the song, many people have claimed that the audience appear to be chanting 'Hoo-rah Rainbow!', but this incorrect. The track was recorded at one of the German shows, in Nuremburg, and what they are actually chanting is 'Zugabe!', which is the German equivalent of the English 'Encore'.

Recorded in Nuremburg – though the vocals were dropped in from another source, generally believed to be another live performance rather than redone in the studio.

Long Live Rock 'n' Roll.

Personnel:
Ritchie Blackmore: guitar
Ronnie James Dio: vocals
David Stone: keyboards
Bob Daisley: bass
Cozy Powell: drums
Record Label: Polydor
Recorded May-July & December 1977, produced by Martin Birch
Release date: April 1978
Highest chart places: UK: 7, USA: 89
Running time: 39:27

Album Facts.

The third and final Dio-era Rainbow studio album was one with a tricky
gestation period, to put it mildly. After the Rising tour of 1976, Blackmore had
summarily sacked Tony Carey and Jimmy Bain – the former allegedly because
his improvisational skills were not good enough. The disagreement with Bain
is less clear, though it cannot have helped that, inveterate practical joker that
he was, Blackmore had on one occasion set fire to his bass player's bed. Which
he was unfortunately in at the time. As Blackmore tells it, Bain leapt up and
hurled the burning sheets out of the window, where they proceeded to set fire
to the Astroturf outside. This may have planted the seeds of a rift.

Whatever the reasons, things became more complicated when, without
replacement bass and keyboard players in the band, they had to go into the
studio to begin recording the new album. Farcically, Carey was hired back
as a session musician to play on the recordings. Mark Clarke was brought
in on bass, but was soon dismissed and had all of his bass parts deleted
by Blackmore, who proceeded to handle bass duties himself for a while.
According to both Clarke and Carey, the main reason for this was that Clarke
liked to play bass with his fingers, whereas Blackmore was insistent he use a
pick.

Australian bass player Bob Daisley, from Widowmaker (who did use a pick!),
was brought in along with Canadian keyboard man David Stone, but in July,
with the album far from complete, the band had to break off for a lengthy
tour of Europe. They reconvened in December to finish off the album, which
eventually appeared in April 1978, almost a year after recording commenced,
and a full nine months since the title track had begun being played live.

The studio used for the recording was the Chateau D'Hereuville in Paris
(the same one christened the 'Chateau D'isaster' by Jethro Tull), an old castle
converted for use as a studio, near Paris. Clarke actually recalls one day when
Powell was playing drums at the bottom of a circular spiral stairwell, while he
was upstairs, completely unable to see him. In keeping with the old, spooky
atmosphere of the place, there were a lot of Ouija boards and séances around,

and certain people have reported the sessions as having become a little unnerving to say the least.

Album Cover.

After the thrilling fantasy extravaganzas of the debut and Rising, the cover of Long Live Rock 'n Roll appeared to an underwhelmed fanbase, consisting of a rather abstract line drawing of the five musicians' heads against a sort of yellowy beige background. The gothic lettered logo was retained, with the same script being used for the album name and also the track titles, somewhat incongruously given the rather prosaic nature of the title and artwork. The rear cover was blank except for the track listing and credits, while the inside gatefold featured a crowd shot, holding up a banner with 'Long live rock 'n' roll' written on it. It is, naturally, monochrome (what else would you expect), but more bizarrely it transpired that the photo wasn't even of a Rainbow crowd. It was taken at a Rush show, and the banner originally read 'Plymouth welcomes RUSH, touring North America 1977', with their 'Starman' logo. Not only was this altered for the Rainbow photo, but the visible Rush T-shirts were also airbrushed out! It remains one of the more bizarre design decisions to have appeared on a major album cover, certainly, as it would not appear to be any easier than simply photographing the band's own audience.

Initial pressings contained an inner sleeve with the lyrics, and we are assured that no Rush songs were harmed during the making of this lyric sheet.

'Long Live Rock 'n' Roll'. (Blackmore, Dio)

The first track on the album gives an indication, backed up by the cover design, that there might be a toning down of the 'wizards and sorcery' element to the music this time out. And indeed this is a much simpler and more direct lyrical message – but what a great track it is for all that. Dio's lyrics, which could have been banal in lesser hands, manage to still sound evocative and interesting, while his delivery somehow makes it not only excusable but well nigh irresistible to sing along and, if the mood strikes, punch the air. It's one of the all time great celebratory anthems, far more rousing than, say 'I Love Rock And Roll', 'Rock And Roll All Night' or 'Long Live Rock'.

Lyrics aside, the music is completely celebratory and infectious, opening with a quick drum fill and then a couple of power chords which usher in the main riff in a similar way to 'Highway Star' six years previously (hard to believe today there was only six years between those two recordings!). Blackmore's solo is tremendous stuff, containing a couple of his trademark licks which almost invite the listener to 'sing along' to it. Unsurprisingly, it took up permanent residence in the set, from the 1977 tour onward, and became a huge crowd favourite. It was released as a single, backed with 'Sensitive To Light', and with its obvious class as a rock song mixed with its massively catchy melodic lines, it really should have been the big hit that they eventually scored with a couple of very much inferior singles. Sadly, the public disagreed, and it stalled at a disappointing Number 33 in the UK chart.

Blackmore played bass on this one himself, with Carey supplying keyboards.

'Lady Of The Lake'. (Blackmore, Dio)

Even if you tried to put Dio on a shorter leash lyrically, this track (and notably, one other) serve to illustrate that you could never neuter his fertile imagination and sense of wonder entirely. The verses are fairly basic driving rock, but the chorus is a big, uplifting pop hook dressed in immaculate hard rock clothing, and it brings the song alive. Lyrically it's a sort of 'fantasy femme fatale' tale, but the words themselves don't matter so much as the way Dio makes them sound. There are a couple of terribly clunky phrases on paper ('with a bubbly turn now the water should turn' for the love of God!), but somehow you don't even notice, so laden with controlled power and drama is his performance, and when he unleashes his full power with the phrase 'diamonds out of the rain' near the end, the effect is glorious. It may only be three minutes and 44 seconds, but it seems longer, and it seems greater.

Blackmore contributes an eerie sounding guitar solo with plenty of slide here, and if you listen closely to the second and third verses (either side of the solo), he is doing the same behind the vocals, producing what on first listen sounds like backing vocals. Again, it's Blackmore and Carey on bass and keyboards respectively here.

'LA Connection'. (Blackmore, Dio)

In contrast with the previous two tracks, we really are in much more prosaic and grounded territory here. The tale of someone needing to get back home after a traumatic experience wherein he loses everything has been reported by members of the Rainbow circle to have been written about Tony Carey's leaving the band for a second time during the recording, when he was last seen heading off to the airport with a suitcase. It would fit, both in subject and timeline, with lines like 'Forty days of cries and moans, I guess I've failed to pass the test / I've been sent away not a thing to say, I'm banished from the fold' – Carey had been perceived by inveterate pranksters Blackmore and Powell to be a bit 'full of himself', and as a result he was tormented mercilessly with pranks and practical jokes.

Slow and plodding, with grinding, insistent guitar work, it is far from the sweeping, widescreen, classically influenced Rainbow epics of yore. In actual fact, It was released as a single – reaching only Number 40 in the UK – backed with 'Lady Of The Lake', and it also became the only track from the album, beyond the already-performed 'Kill The King' and title track, to make it into the live set, though it didn't stay in there very long. Blackmore is on bass again here, but David Stone finally gets in on the action with the piano heard toward the end.

'Gates Of Babylon'. (Blackmore, Dio)

For many people, this is the real centrepiece of the album. The only true, lengthy epic in the proud Rainbow tradition, it even utilises the talents of the

Bavarian String Ensemble to create a little bit of the old 'Stargazer' magic. The mysterious, cryptic tale of the protagonist seemingly having his soul taken from him away to hell was allegedly inspired after a séance that the crew held on the 1977 tour, but whatever the genesis of the lyric, it is one of Dio's very best ever.

Blackmore's music has that 'Eastern', Arabic influenced sound to it again, so beloved by him. It propels the song along superbly, leaving the listener slightly disorientated and taken aback. Running to almost seven minutes, there is even time for a big-sounding midsection with some slow, intense power-chords and magnificent guitar work, which David Stone is adamant that he was responsible for. He claims that he worked on that mid-section with Martin Birch over the course of a night, and he was assured by manager Bruce Payne that he would get a publishing credit, but instead he got a cheque as settlement. He says the reason he was given was that it was 'too much paperwork'!

The track was never played live, owing to what Blackmore described as being, once again, because it simply didn't sound right. In that same interview wherein he spoke about the reasons for dropping 'Stargazer' from the set, he continues: ''Gates Of Babylon' was another, like 'Stargazer', that never worked when we tried to play it live either, you see. We did try it actually, but it just ended up a mess, to be honest with you, so we left it alone.' Dio did perform the song with his own band in later years, as indeed he did with 'Stargazer'.

The track was the last to be finished for the album, being recorded at the December '77 sessions, and the bass and keyboards are by the actual credited musicians, Daisley and Stone. In fact, Stone contributes a short keyboard intro which comes across superbly well, and Daisley is also key in terms of powering the track along. It is the standout on the album by some distance, and the only song where Dio really gives full and free rein to his imagination. By the next album he would be gone, and the path towards a much more commercial sound would spread out invitingly for Blackmore, who took it.

'Kill The King'. (Blackmore, Dio, Powell)

This one seems a bit odd to include, as everyone had known it from the high-adrenalin live version released a year before, and it had been played for a year before that, since the release of *Rising*. In truth, it loses a little bit in power from that live recording, but the guitar solo on here almost makes up for that, and it is a clearer and more polished recording. Still a great song. Once again, Daisley and Stone are both present and correct here.

'The Shed (Subtle)'. (Blackmore, Dio, Powell)

It's safe to say that this simplistic, stomping rocker isn't one of early Rainbow's best-remembered works. This is surely the sort of lyrical subject matter that Dio was tiring of having to write when he fell out with Blackmore and departed after this album. The riff clumps along like a sort of third cousin of 'God Of Thunder' by Kiss, while Dio informs us he is, variously, like a freight train, feeling no pain, street walkin', night stalkin' and, most dramatically, not talkin'.

Perhaps he liked to be quiet and reflective while he was walkin' and stalkin'. In truth, while it isn't the first poor effort Rainbow produced, it is a shame to hear the man behind lyrical masterpieces such as 'Temple Of The King' and 'Stargazer' reduced to this. And Cozy Powell being limited to a simplistic thumping accompaniment is like hiring Roger Dean to paint your skirting boards. What his writing credit was for we can only surmise.

The odd title is allegedly a reference to Chelsea FC's football stadium Stamford Bridge, where the hardcore and those of a violent persuasion would occupy an area behind the goal known as The Shed. Apparently, so the story goes, Blackmore was a Chelsea fan growing up, and Dio titled it as a bit of an in-joke. The 'Subtle' subtitle supposedly refers to the solo guitar introduction.

'Sensitive To Light'. (Blackmore, Dio)

Another depressingly mundane Dio lyric, with him relating a tale of a woman who is trouble whenever he gets involved with her. In that regard, it is no better than 'The Shed', but it is at least musically a lot more energised. In fact it's a decent, catchy, uptempo rock song. No more, no less.

'Rainbow Eyes'. (Blackmore, Dio)

The closing track on the album is a completely unexpected departure from the previous two tracks, with the instrumentation mainly coming from Blackmore with the addition of violin, viola, cello and flute providing accompaniment. Clearly a nod back to 'Catch The Rainbow', it is the clearest example yet of Blackmore's love of medieval musical influences, and it is inarguably a lovely melody. The main issue with the track is that it doesn't develop, and while it starts exquisitely, it struggles to sustain itself over its more than seven minute duration. Strangely, Blackmore apparently did not care for Dio's vocal in this song, and revisited it again years later with his Blackmore's Night project, but listening now it is hard to see how Ronnie could have improved his performance on this.

Lyrically, it was Dio's ode to his wife Wendy (they married in 1978), whose deteriorating relationship with Blackmore did not help with the issue of Ronnie's departure. Wendy supposedly had eyes which seemed to change colour, and he referred to them as her 'rainbow eyes'. In a way, a beautiful and reflective song such as this was the perfect way for Ronnie's Rainbow tenure to end. If the final song on his final album had been 'The Shed', it would be wrong. There are conflicting accounts of his departure from Ritchie, Wendy and other band members and associates. Some say he was fired, others that he walked; some say she stoked his own ego and caused clashes, others that he was being shepherded towards a commercial path that he refused to take. Whatever the truth of it, one of hard rock music's greatest ever partnerships was at an end, and the next album would start to usher in a whole new era.

Down To Earth.

Personnel:
Ritchie Blackmore: guitar
Graham Bonnet: vocals
Don Airey: keyboards
Roger Glover: bass
Cozy Powell: drums
Record Label: Polydor
Recorded April-July 1979, produced by Roger Glover
Release date: July 1979
Highest chart places: UK: 6, USA: 66
Running time: 36:05

Album facts.

So, Dio was out. And in his place was Graham Bonnet, all short hair, Hawaiian shirts and sunglasses. The change was dramatically evident. Don Airey came in to replace David Stone on keyboards, while the biggest surprise was the return to Blackmore's orbit of Roger Glover on bass, who also produced the album. In an interview with the author, he spoke about this time, and how he reconnected with Blackmore after his sacking from Purple: 'I met him again three years later, when he was working on the *Rainbow Rising* album in a studio in Germany, and he was friendly enough. He said he wanted to play me a song, so he played me 'Stargazer', in the studio, loud, and I was utterly blown away. I said "Ritchie, this is a masterpiece" – and from that, after the band imploded and got rebuilt a while later, I got the invitation to produce the *Down To Earth* album. While working on it, I was writing songs with Ritchie, and playing on a session basis, and by the time the album was finished I got asked to join. It was a good career opportunity, and I'm glad I did it. I'm an opportunist – and it was a great opportunity. Why have a grudge against someone who's such a great artist? I gave him a pass, and decided to let him get away with it.'

Before the recording commenced, and the line-up became finalised, there were other candidates. In a bizarre move one night around Christmas 1978, Blackmore turned up at Ian Gillan's house and invited him to join, over copious amounts of vodka. Despite the convivial atmosphere, Gillan turned down the offer, which is probably best for the sanity of all concerned. A bass player named Clive Chaman was briefly hired, as was Jack Green, formerly with The Pretty Things. Pete Goalby, who had been in Trapeze with Hughes, was considered as Dio's replacement, but did not work out. The actual recording was again at a French chateau, this time the Chateau Pelly de Cornfield in the south of the country, with the Maison Rouge ('Red House') mobile studio. The exception to this is Bonnet's vocals, which were recorded separately, after the rest of the recording was done, at Kingdom Studios in Long Island – he had complained in France that he did not like recording his vocals unless he was in an actual recording studio.

Album Cover.

The front cover of the album, in an odd echo of the *Fireball* cover, showed the words 'Down To Earth' coming out of a planet (presumably Earth), with a tail behind it in rainbow colours, in a painting by sci-fi artist Ron Walotsky. The back shows the same planet, with simply the tracklisting and credits. There was no gatefold, but there was an insert with some band photos. All in all, an uninspiring package. The label design was rather strange, with one side having all of the tracks listed and the other, for no discernible reason, featuring the Rising cover image of the fist holding the rainbow, complete with original gothic logo.

'All Night Long'. (Blackmore, Glover)

If the new direction hadn't been anticipated before, here it was writ large for all to see in this opening track. A straightforward fast, riff-driven rocker with a huge catchy chorus, it was released as a single (with non-album instrumental 'Weiss Heim' on the flip) and reached Number Five in the UK singles chart. Lyrically - Glover penned all of the lyrics now, after Dio's departure, not, you will note, Bonnet - it was basic and in places somewhat crass or amusing in a deliberately 'offensive' way, depending on your viewpoint – the line 'don't know about your brain but you look all right' got up certain people's noses considerably in 1979. A decent, if intellectually unchallenging, start to the album. Released as the follow-up single to 'Since You've Been Gone', it was another big hit in the UK, reaching number five.

'Eyes Of The World'. (Blackmore, Glover)

This piece, stretching to just under seven minutes, is the last nod to the old 'epic' Rainbow – at least, until the 1990s return of the Rainbow brand and the album *Stranger In Us All*. Glover conjures up an excellent lyric concerning the consequences of man's actions ('if only you could see the tears of pain, in the eyes of the world') which Bonnet delivers superbly in his best performance on the album. Musically, well, we're seeing the ghost of 'Stargazer' here as that glorious Eastern-sounding trademark Rainbow 'epic' feel is reanimated from the grave and sent out lumbering across the fields. It's nearly seven minutes long, but in actual fact is shorter than that as the first minute and a bit is taken up by a keyboard intro which seems to be borrowing a little from Holst's 'Mars – The Bringer Of War'. All credit where it is due – this is a tremendous song, and offered real hope for the future of the band. It was ultimately a false hope, but it seemed to be a new dawn just for a moment. And the guitar solo is exceptional.

'No Time To Lose'. (Blackmore, Glover)

Ah well, that was nice while it lasted. Unfortunately we're back to the basics again with this sub-four minute rocker. It's fast, it's a little catchy and Bonnet is enthusiastic by the sound of it. That's about it for the 'plus' column though, unfortunately. The song is unremarkable in the extreme, and there is little to raise it above the slightly depressing norm.

'Makin' Love'. (Blackmore, Glover)

Now then. After tracks one and three of this album, and with this title, what are you expecting here? Exactly. Well, surprisingly our expectations are subverted and exceeded in this case, as this is far from the piece of chest-beating bluster that the title points to. Opening with a beautiful guitar and keyboard intro which almost seems as if we are going to be treated to another 'Temple Of The King' or 'Catch The Rainbow' (no, we can't get THAT lucky), the song itself opens with a chugging shuffle rhythm from Blackmore and some quite soulful vocals from Bonnet. The chorus ('How can I deny my heart...') has quite a lovely melodic touch to it, and the song as a whole straddles the melodic and the biting edge with some skill. There is a twice repeated section ('Don't believe that I'm a liar...') which sounds uncomfortably close to Kiss, but it doesn't compromise things overly. Blackmore's guitar solo is completely 'by numbers', sounding as if he could have done it in his sleep, but overall it's a surprisingly pleasant song.

'Since You Been Gone'. (Ballard)

Now here we have the real bone of contention: the big hit single (number 6 in the UK) version of Russ Ballard's song. This was the apex of Rainbow's commercial approach up to this point, and the piece which really upset legions of old-school fans across the world, while simultaneously raking in equally large numbers of new ones. Listening to the track now is a rather conflicting experience: it is hard not to hold a strong dislike and resentment for everything the track represented, but at the same time it is a very strong and superbly written song for what it is, and the band deliver it extremely well. The melody is sublime in the way it gets its hooks into the listener's brain while avoiding the trap of being simultaneously irritating, but by the same token it's about as far from the Silver Mountain as it was possible to get.

Cozy Powell was reportedly very vocal in his distaste for the song when it was recorded, refusing to do any further takes as it represented everything to him that Rainbow should not have been. He did apparently soften in his public comments about it after its huge success, which is understandable, but on balance let's go with his first assessment. Catchy and well played it certainly was, but the Rainbow which made us dream and gave us chills it certainly wasn't. And if you couldn't trust Cozy, who could you trust? Down To Earth indeed.

One thing that could be said for the song, however, is that it was better than the other, later, Ballard cover by the band, 'I Surrender'. Now that really was a low point.

'Love's No Friend'. (Blackmore, Glover)

The track that most people seem to forget or overlook on the album, this is a slow-burning, grinding bluesy rocker. It doesn't really resonate with Bonnet's chief vocal strengths (like Dio, and unlike Coverdale, the man didn't have the blues anywhere in him), and ultimately comes and goes without leaving too much of a footprint. Odds are you won't hate it but you won't love it either.

'Danger Zone'. (Blackmore, Glover)

Getting towards the end of the album, we have quite the improvement here. A churning, insistent rhythm from Blackmore underpins a busy, urgent sounding lyrical delivery from Bonnet, with the verses finished by a rather tasty ascending melody. A nice, rocking, catchy chorus adds to things while an unexpectedly retro-Rainbow 'Eastern-sounding' instrumental break complete with nice keyboards from Don Airey make this one of the highlights of the album. A good time for things to take a bit of an upturn, just as the second side of the record was threatening to peter out a little, and a nice hors-d'oeuvre before the meat of the albums final track arrives.

'Lost In Hollywood'. (Blackmore, Glover, Powell)

Ah, this is better! The final track on the album turns out to be absolutely first-class. A cracking, fast-paced rocker with a pretty good lyric, concerning being stuck in LA away from other important things. Bonnet is on great form here, with his trademark 'Bonnet melody' on the 'Last time I saw your face' part lending support to the claim that he added the vocal melodies himself and perhaps should have got some songwriting credit; listening to the album as a whole his stamp is all over it in that regard, often to the betterment of the song. It's an attribute he shares with Dio, along with his 'blues-less' delivery, and in the final analysis marks him down as a reasonable choice as his, admittedly short-lived, successor. Soon after this album, and the resulting tour, he was gone to be replaced by the less impressively-voiced if more suitably image-conscious Joe Lynn Turner, and the commercial side of the band would gain the true upper hand.

This would also be the parting shot of Cozy Powell on a Rainbow album, and as such it is nice to see him getting one last writing credit. Certainly his drum work on the track is phenomenal, driving it on like a Japanese bullet train. He would be missed, firstly by the band and later by the wider world after his tragic demise in a car accident.

Related Songs.

'Bad Girl'. (Blackmore, Glover)

The B-side of 'Since You Been Gone'. There is honestly little more to be said about this plodding pop-rocker-by-numbers. It's pure B-side material, with 'throwaway' written through it like a stick of rock. Don't bother seeking it out. The guitar solo is better than the song.

'Weiss Heim'. (Blackmore)

The B-side to 'All Night Long'. This, on the other hand, is much more worthwhile. A beautifully expressive, evocative instrumental, it features some of the finest and most restrained Blackmore guitar work for some time. It was recorded a few months after the album, which is a shame as its inclusion would have improved it quite significantly, especially if at the expense of some of the deadwood such as 'No Time To Lose' or 'Love's No Friend'. A great shame that this was thrown away on a B-side, but the other side of that coin (the B-side of the coin, if you will) is that fans of a certain age will remember this spending a lot of time playing on 1980 jukeboxes, as it received a lot of play from people who either did not have the single, and wanted to hear it, or else had the single and wanted other people to hear it. The title ('White Home') comes from the name of Blackmore's house in Long Island at the time.

Roundup – Odds, Sods, Live and Video

Live Material

We've already covered the core live albums released during the lifespan of the bands here, of course, but let's take a quick look at some of the other material released featuring the period covered herein. There have been a lot of 'official bootleg' releases in recent times of complete shows by Marks II, III and IV, of variable quality. These are often soundboard recordings, and therefore decent quality in themselves, but there are instances sometimes when the vocals may be too loud in the mix etc. I won't cover all of these, but suffice it to say that if you want the complete, unedited shows that contributed to *Made In Japan*, *Made In Europe* and even Rainbow's *On Stage*, they are mostly there to find easily.

The first live album to appear after the initial Deep Purple split in 1976 was the ill-starred *Last Concert In Japan*, which appeared a year later in March 1977. Recorded in December 1975 in Tokyo, it is well documented that Tommy Bolin's playing was severely compromised after he had reportedly fallen asleep on his arm the previous night when he was high. It has also been claimed that he missed a vein with a needle, and caused an abscess rendering his left arm almost useless. Whatever the reason, the result is painfully apparent on the resulting album, which nonetheless has some merit as a show simply because of the superhuman efforts Lord made to cover for the guitar parts, and also the sterling work of Paice and Coverdale. Nevertheless, badly recorded and musically compromised as it was, it should never have appeared. It is notable for live versions of 'You Keep On Moving', a shortened 'Soldier Of Fortune' and an excellent rendition of Bolin's song 'Wild Dogs'. The cover indicated a performance of 'Woman From Tokyo' which turned out to be merely a short jam during Lord's keyboard solo, and which infuriated fans who, possibly quite rightly, interpreted it as a record company tactic.

A while later in 1980, the double album *Deep Purple In Concert* appeared, containing a disc apiece from 1970 and 1972 recorded for the BBC. There are good performances, but it is inessential – the 1972 show features the familiar *Machine Head* stuff, albeit with a rare performance of 'Never Before' (plus an even rarer one of 'maybe I'm A Leo' which was omitted from the original vinyl), while the 1970 album features near-20 minute workouts of 'Wring That Neck' and 'Mandrake Root', plus the usual 'Speed King' and 'Child In Time'. It was more valuable as a document at the time when these performances were never heard outside of bootlegs. An album called *Live In London* appeared in 1982, featuring a 1974 show from the Burn tour, but is chiefly interesting nowadays for performances of 'Might Just Take Your Life' and 'Lay Down Stay Down'. A Mk IV show from Long Beach in 1976 was released later under the odd title of *On The Wings Of A Russian Foxbat* – while it is much better than *Last Concert In Japan*, it is still not the greatest representation of the Bolin line-up: they were notoriously inconsistent live, largely due to the often wayward genius that was Bolin himself.

Compilations

There were a few notable compilation albums which appeared within the scope of this book, most of which actually had something of note about them. The most widespread deep Purple compilation of the 1970s in the UK was without doubt the Mk II collection *24 Carat Purple*, which appeared in 1975. The album rounded up some favourites, with the *Made In Japan* versions of 'Smoke On The Water', 'Child In Time' and 'Strange Kind Of Woman' joining the studio versions of 'Speed King', 'Fireball', 'Never Before' and 'Woman From Tokyo', but the real bait which made this album an essential part of so many record collections in the mid-'70s was the inclusion of the live 'Black Night' from the Japan encores. To increase its enormous circulation at the time was the fact that it appeared priced roughly half that of a regular album, with the result that penniless schoolboys the length and breadth of Great Britain flocked to buy it! Its cheap and cheerful laminated gold sleeve had a series of monochrome thumbnail pictures of all of the purple albums from *Shades* to *Stormbringer*, with one extra picture of a mysterious album entitled *Purple Passages*, which turned out, upon further investigation (not easy in those pre-internet times) to be a US double disc compilation of Mk I material released in 1972.

The first Purple collection to include Mk I and Mk II material was the self-explanatory double *Deep Purple Mark 1 And 2* in December 1973. The main point of interest musically here was the inclusion of the non-album single 'Emmaretta', which was the only place to get that particular track on album at the time, but another significant thing about the album is that it is widely believed to be the first time the famous 'Mark' designations were used.

There were two further compilations of significance in the period we are looking at. Firstly the album *Powerhouse* in 1977, which rounded up the live material played before the Concerto performance in 1969, and also rarities like 'Painted Horse' and 'When A Blind Man Cries'. It is interesting, but the live performances are not definitive. Following this a year later was *Singles 'A's and 'B's*, which was interesting as the only way to easily get hold of 'Hallelujah'. The hideously titled *When We Rock We Rock, And When We Roll We Roll* was a bizarre single disc mix of Mk I and II material and a waste of time, while the 1980 *Mk II Deep Purple Singles* again rounded up the increasingly less rare 'When A Blind Man Cries' and 'Painted Horse'. The cover designs of these last two albums were so appalling they made one wonder if they were actually designed by the weeping blind man from the song.

Video

Decent quality, official DVD footage of 1970s Purple performances is not thick on the ground. There was a DVD entitled *Scandinavian Nights* or *In Concert 1973/73*, which featured a 1972 show in Copenhagen, together with some additional material from a New York show in 1973. There are some great performances on these (the Copenhagen show was also released on CD), but visually it is lacking, largely because the Copenhagen footage is in black and white (what was it with this band and monochrome?)

If it was colour you were after, however, that was available in spades on the video, and later DVD, of the 1974 California Jam show. Famously, the Purple appearance was delayed after Blackmore locked himself in his trailer, refusing to play until the sun had gone down, as had been agreed. When he eventually was forced to appear it was with a clearly simmering rage barely below the surface. Toward the end of an excellent set – performed, interestingly, in front of a backdrop of a rainbow – that simmering fury turned into incandescent rage when, during the 'Space Truckin' jam, a foolhardy cameraman dared to approach Blackmore's part of the stage, against his express wishes. What follows is a rampage of destruction which beggars belief. First Blackmore attacks the hapless cameraman – and his camera – with his guitar, throwing the remains of the mangled instrument into the crowd. He then has his speaker cabinets doused in petrol and sets them alight. The resultant explosion, clearly bigger than even he anticipated, almost sets him on fire, blows Ian Paice's glasses off and sends the cabinets hurtling off the stage. The band continue to play.

An interesting footnote to this is that the film of this climactic California Jam madness can be seen playing in the van during the tornado-chasing 1996 movie *Twister*. Whether this is any sort of in-joke or homage to the *Stormbringer* album title is unknown, but not unreasonable.

Epilogue – What Came Next

Of course, both Deep Purple and Rainbow continued significantly beyond the scope of this book – though in the eyes of many, including the author, never with quite the same impact .

Rainbow recruited singer Joe Lynn Turner, a man who looked more like a rock frontman than Graham Bonnet but had a much smoother and less interesting voice, and the band's sound drifted squarely into a more commercial rock direction over the course of the albums *Difficult To Cure*, *Straight Between The Eyes* and *Bent Out Of Shape*. There were still fine tracks, such as 'Street Of Dreams' and the Beethoven adaptation 'Difficult To Cure', but the magic had gone. Rainbow ground to a halt in 1984 when the unthinkable happened – Deep Purple Mk II reformed, Blackmore and Gillan and all.

In the intervening years, the other various Purple members had not been idle, with David Coverdale launching the massively successful – and still ongoing – Whitesnake, in whose ranks both Paice and Lord did time before the Purple call came again. They had also been in the short-lived Paice Ashton Lord project, whose unremarkable *Malice In Wonderland* album proved their sole legacy. Ian Gillan, meanwhile, had followed up the somewhat jazzy Ian Gillan Band with the straight hard-rocking approach of the band Gillan, who hit a rich seam of popularity right from the debut *Mr Universe* album. Ronnie James Dio stepped out of Rainbow into an equally successful stint with Black Sabbath, who also had Cozy Powell in their ranks later, though not at the same time. He went on to front his own band, Dio, until his untimely demise in 2010, with two further short spells with the Sabbath guys interspersed. The Black Sabbath connection was further added to by Bob Daisley joining Ozzy Osbourne's original Blizzard Of Ozz band. Glenn Hughes also briefly stepped through the revolving door of Sabbath members in the 1980s, for the heavily criticised *Seventh Star* album. After leaving Purple, he released a straight soul/funk album *Play Me Out* before taking time out to conquer his personal demons and finally returning to the fray with a series of excellent recordings up to the present day, veering between the rock and funk extremes and all points in between.

The Purple reformation was a huge success right off the bat, with a spectacularly successful world tour and the excellent *Perfect Strangers* album, which contained genuinely classic material such as 'Knocking At Your Back Door', 'Wasted Sunsets' and the epic title track – the latter arguably the only dyed-in-the-wool classic from the 1980s onward to achieve the fan status of the '70s material. Following this, however, things began to steadily unravel, with the disappointing follow-up album, *The House Of Blue Light* (complete with painfully 'nostalgic' title) being followed by the utterly unsurprising departure of Gillan again, after relations with – take a wild guess – Blackmore became once again untenable. Uninspired Rainbow man Joe Lynn Turner was drafted in for the *Slaves And Masters* album, which managed to sound rather unfortunately like another in the run of '80s Rainbow albums. Nobody was exactly stunned when Turner lasted only for the one album, but they certainly were surprised when Gillan returned again. The resulting album *The Battle Rages On* was better than its reputation might suggest, containing some top quality cuts in the shape of the title track, 'Anya' and 'Ramshackle Man', but Blackmore (who would derisively refer to it as 'The Cattle Grazes On') became more and more unsettled, quitting halfway through the resulting tour, after a particularly fraught gig in Birmingham (filmed and recorded as it happened) when he did not even appear on stage until near the end of opener 'Highway Star'. Joe Satriani stepped in as a temporary live replacement to finish the tour.

American guitarist Steve Morse became the permanent replacement for Blackmore in 1994, and has now (depressingly to those of us of a certain age who view the '90s as if they were last week) played many more Purple shows than Blackmore ever did. Their albums, from *Purpendicular* through to the most recent *Infinity* have all been of a good standard, but many would argue lacking the touch of uniqueness that the 'Blackmore effect' had provided, for good or bad. Latter day Purple have been professional, well-rehearsed and have introduced many old songs vetoed by Blackmore into the live set ('Hard Lovin' Man', 'Fools', 'Pictures Of Home', 'Woman From Tokyo', 'When A Blind Man Cries' etc), but somehow have never had that sense of danger, or of 'playing on the edge of a cliff' that was once the case. Jon Lord tragically passed away in 2012 from cancer, and was replaced by much-travelled keyboard man Don Airey.

Following his final (at time of writing at least!) departure from the Purple ranks, Ritchie Blackmore reformed Rainbow with an entirely new line-up, including singer Doogie White, for the strong 1995 album *Stranger In Us All*. Disbanding after one tour, however, that iteration never realised its full potential, and Blackmore went on to form Blackmore's Night, along with his singer wife Candice, indulging his love of medieval inspired music and a more folky direction. There were still rock elements in the mix however, and over their 20 year career it could easily be argued that Blackmore's Night have possessed more of the spirit of that very first Rainbow album than the later, slicker, Rainbow machine.

The Rainbow banner was reactivated one final time in 2016, with Blackmore assembling a new line-up to play a short series of shows (plus a handful more the following year) to play a set drawing from both his Purple and Rainbow history. The shows were widely criticised for being poorly rehearsed, and for Blackmore himself suffering from hand problems, but if nothing else it was a chance to see him performing tracks like 'Child In Time' and 'Stargazer' in the same show. And that is something which cannot be overlooked.

Afterword – The Ultimate Playlist

Finally, and just to close things, here is a suggested 30-track playlist of the greatest Purple and Rainbow material from the period covered in this book. Purely the author's opinion, of course!

Wring That Neck
Anthem
Blind
Hallelujah
Hard Lovin' man
Child In Time (live version)
Fireball
No One Came
Highway Star
Pictures Of Home
Smoke On The Water (live version)
Black Night (live version)
Woman From Tokyo
Our Lady
Burn
Mistreated
Stormbringer
The Gypsy
Soldier Of Fortune
Comin' Home
You Keep On Moving
Man On The Silver Mountain
Catch The Rainbow
Temple Of The King
Stargazer
A Light In The Black
Still I'm Sad (live version)
Long Live Rock And Roll
Gates Of Babylon
Eyes Of The World

Bibliography

Bloom, J., *Black Night: Ritchie Blackmore* (Omnibus, 2008)

Gillan, I., *Ian Gillan: The Autobiography Of Deep Purple's Singer* (John Blake, 1998)

Prato, G., *The Other Side Of Rainbow* (CIPP, 2016)

Robinson, S and Clare, S., *Wait For The Ricochet* (Easy On The Eye Books, 2013)

Popoff, M., *Sail Away: Whitesnake's Fantastic Voyage* (Soundcheck Books, 2015)

Would you like to write for Sonicbond Publishing?

At Sonicbond Publishing we are always on the look-out for authors, particularly for our two main series:

On Track. Mixing fact with in depth analysis, the On Track series examines the work of a particular musical artist or group. All genres are considered from easy listening and jazz to 60s soul to 90s pop, via rock and metal.

On Screen. This series looks at the world of film and television. Subjects considered include directors, actors and writers, as well as entire television and film series. As with the On Track series, we balance fact with analysis.

While professional writing experience would, of course, be an advantage the most important qualification is to have real enthusiasm and knowledge of your subject. First-time authors are welcomed, but the ability to write well in English is essential.

Sonicbond Publishing has distribution throughout Europe and North America, and all books are also published in E-book form. Authors will be paid a royalty based on sales of their book.

Further details are available from www.sonicbondpublishing.co.uk. To contact us, complete the contact form there or email info@sonicbondpublishing.co.uk

Also from Sonicbond Publishing

On Track series
Emerson Lake and Palmer
Mike Goode ISBN: 978-1-78952-000-2

Queen
Andrew Wild ISBN: 978-1-78952-003-3

Yes
Stephen Lambe ISBN: 978-1-78952-001-9

Blue Oyster Cult
Jacob Holm Lupo ISBN: 978-1-78952-007-1

The Beatles
Andrew Wild ISBN: 978-1-78952-009-5

Roy Wood and the Move
James R Turner ISBN: 978-1-78952-008-8

Genesis
Stuart MacFarlane ISBN: 978-1-78952-005-7

Jethro Tull
Jordan Blum ISBN: 978-1-78952-016-3

The Rolling Stones 1963-80
Steve Pilkington ISBN: 978-1-78952-017-0

On Screen series
Carry On...
Stephen Lambe ISBN: 978-1-78952-004-0

Seinfeld
Stephen Lambe ISBN: 978-1-78952-012-5

Audrey Hepburn
Ellen Cheshire ISBN: 978-1-78952-011-8

Powell and Pressburger
Sam Proctor ISBN: 978-1-78952-013-2

Dad's Army
Huw Lloyd- Jones ISBN: 978-1-78952-015-6

and many more to come!